# Family

BLOOMSBURY KITCHEN LIBRARY

# Family

BLOOMSBURY BOOKS
LONDON

This edition published 1995 by Bloomsbury Books,
an imprint of The Godfrey Cave Group,
42 Bloomsbury Street, London, WC1B 3QJ.

All rights reserved. No part of this publication may be reproduced,
stored in a retrieval system, or transmitted, in any form or by any
means, electronic, mechanical, photocopying, recording or otherwise
without the prior permission of the copyright holder.

© 1995 Time-Life Books B.V.

ISBN 1 85471 508 9

Printed and bound in Great Britain.

# Contents

# Wheat Berry Muffins

Makes 12
muffins

Working time:
about 20
minutes

Total time:
about 2 hours

Per muffin:
Calories
210
Protein
7g
Cholesterol
45mg
Total fat
4g
Saturated fat
1g
Sodium
210mg

| | | | | | | |
|---|---|---|---|---|---|---|
| 100 g | wheat berries | 3½ oz | ¼ tsp | salt | | ¼ tsp |
| 175 g | plain flour | 6 oz | 2 | eggs | | 2 |
| 125 g | wholemeal flour | 4 oz | 90 g | honey | | 3 oz |
| 60 g | dried skimmed milk | 2 oz | 2 tbsp | safflower oil | | 2 tbsp |
| 1 tsp | baking powder | 1 tsp | 35 cl | buttermilk | | 12 fl oz |
| 1 tsp | bicarbonate of soda | 1 tsp | 75 g | raisins | | 2½ oz |
| ½ tsp | ground cinnamon | ½ tsp | | | | |

Bring ¼ litre (8 fl oz) of water to the boil in a saucepan and then add the wheat berries. Reduce the heat to low, cover the pan and simmer the kernels until they are tender—1½ to 2 hours. If the wheat berries absorb all the water before they finish cooking, pour in more water, 4 tablespoons at a time, to keep them from burning. Drain them and set them aside.

Preheat the oven to 190°C (375°F or Mark 5). Lightly oil 12 cups in a muffin tin or deep bun tin. Stir together the two flours, the dried milk, baking powder, bicarbonate of soda, cinnamon and salt in a bowl. In another bowl, mix the eggs with the honey and the oil and stir in the buttermilk. Combine the egg mixture with the flour mixture and stir just until they are blended; do not overmix. Fold in the wheat berries and raisins.

Spoon the batter into the cups in the tin, filling each one no more than two-thirds full. Bake the muffins until they are golden-brown—16 to 18 minutes. Serve the muffins immediately.

# Irish Soda Scones with Currants and Caraway Seeds

Makes 24
scones

Working time:
about 15
minutes

Total time:
about 30
minutes

Per scone:
Calories
85
Protein
2g
Cholesterol
13mg
Total fat
2g
Saturated fat
1g
Sodium
120mg

| | | | | | |
|---|---|---|---|---|---|
| **300 g** | plain flour | **10 oz** | **¼ tsp** | salt | **¼ tsp** |
| **125 g** | wholemeal flour | **4 oz** | **15 g** | cold unsalted butter | **½ oz** |
| **2 tbsp** | caster sugar | **2 tbsp** | **1 tbsp** | caraway seeds | **1 tbsp** |
| **2 tsp** | baking powder | **2 tsp** | **1** | egg | **1** |
| **1 tsp** | bicarbonate of soda | **1 tsp** | **¼ litre** | buttermilk | **8 fl oz** |
| **30 g** | cold unsalted polyunsaturated margarine | **1 oz** | **75 g** | currants | **2½ oz** |
| | | | **2 tbsp** | semi-skimmed milk | **2 tbsp** |

Preheat the oven to 180°C (350°F or Mark 4). In a bowl, combine the two flours, the sugar, baking powder, bicarbonate of soda and salt. Using a pastry blender or two knives, cut in the margarine and butter until the mixture resembles coarse meal. In another bowl, whisk the caraway seeds, egg and buttermilk together. Stir the buttermilk mixture and the currants into the flour mixture. (The dough will become too stiff to stir before all the flour is mixed in.)

Turn the dough out on to a lightly floured surface and knead it gently just until the flour is incorporated. Roll or pat the dough so that it is about 2 cm (¾ inch) thick. Cut out rounds with a 5 cm (2 inch) biscuit cutter or the rim of a small glass, and place the scones on an ungreased baking sheet. Gather up the scraps of dough, form them into a ball, and repeat the process. Brush the scones with the milk and cut a cross on the top of each with the tip of a sharp knife or a pair of scissors. Bake the scones until they are golden-brown—about 15 minutes. Serve the scones while they are hot.

# Banana Crème Caramel

Serves 8

Working time: about 45 minutes

Total time: about 3 hours and 15 minutes

Calories 160
Protein 3g
Cholesterol 70mg
Total fat 2g
Saturated fat 1g
Sodium 35mg

| | | |
|---|---|---|
| **165 g** | sugar | **5½ oz** |
| **4 tsp** | fresh lemon juice | **4 tsp** |
| **¼ litre** | semi-skimmed milk | **8 fl oz** |
| **2** | eggs | **2** |
| **1 tbsp** | dark rum | **1 tbsp** |
| **1 tsp** | pure vanilla extract | **1 tsp** |
| **¼ tsp** | ground cardamom or cinnamon | **¼ tsp** |
| **¼ litre** | puréed banana (from 2 to 3 bananas) | **8 fl oz** |
| **2** | bananas, peeled and diagonally sliced | **2** |

Preheat the oven to 170°C (325°F or Mark 3).

First, caramelize a 1 litre (2 pint) souffle dish. In a small heavy saucepan, combine 100 g (3½ oz) sugar, 1 teaspoon of the lemon juice and 3 tablespoons of water. Cook over medium-high heat until the syrup browns and caramelizes. Immediately remove the saucepan from the heat. Quickly pour the caramel into the souffle dish. Using oven gloves, tilt the dish around to coat the bottom and about 2.5 cm (1 inch) of the sides.

For the custard, put the milk into a heavy saucepan over medium heat. As soon as it boils, remove from the heat and set it aside.

Whisk the eggs with the remaining sugar, then add the rum, vanilla extract, cardamom, puréed banana, and remaining lemon juice. Stirring constantly, pour in the hot milk. Transfer to the caramelized dish.

Set the dish in a roasting pan filled with 2.5 cm (1 inch) of water. Bake until a knife inserted in the centre comes out clean. Remove from the hot-water bath and cool to room temperature, then refrigerate for 2 hours.

To unmould, invert a serving plate over the top of the dish, then turn both over together. Garnish with banana slices before serving.

# Vanilla Custard with Yogurt and Apricots

Serves 10

Working time:
about 30
minutes

Total time:
about 1 hour
and 30
minutes

Calories
205
Protein
6g
Cholesterol
65mg
Total fat
3g
Saturated fat
2g
Sodium
110mg

| | | | | | | |
|---|---|---|---|---|---|---|
| 125 g | dried apricots, coarsely chopped | 4 oz | 5 cm | length of vanilla pod, split | 2 inch |
| 200 g | plus 1 tbsp sugar | 7 oz | | lengthwise, or 1 tsp pure | |
| 6 tbsp | cornflour | 6 tbsp | | vanilla extract | |
| $\frac{1}{8}$ tsp | salt | $\frac{1}{8}$ tsp | 2 | eggs, beaten | 2 |
| 1 litre | semi-skimmed milk | 1$\frac{1}{4}$ pints | 17.5 cl | plain low-fat yogurt | 6 fl oz |

Combine the apricots with 12.5 cl (4 fl oz) of water and 1 tablespoon of the sugar in a glass bowl. Cover the bowl and microwave the mixture on high, stopping midway to stir it, until the apricots are tender—4 to 6 minutes. Purée the mixture in a food processor or a blender, then return the purée to the bowl. Cover the bowl and refrigerate it.

Combine the cornflour, salt and the remaining sugar in a small bowl. Pour the milk into a 2 litre (3$\frac{1}{2}$ pint) glass bowl and add the cornflour mixture. Whisk the mixture until the cornflour is completely dissolved. Add the vanilla pod, if you are using it. Microwave the mixture on high, stopping once or twice to stir it, until the milk is hot—about 8 minutes.

If you are using the vanilla pod, remove it from the milk and scrape the seeds inside it into the milk. Discard the pod.

Whisk about 12.5 cl (4 fl oz) of the hot milk into the eggs. Immediately whisk the egg-milk mixture—and the vanilla extract, if you are using it—into the remaining hot milk. Microwave the mixture on high for 3 minutes. Whisk the mixture and continue cooking it on high, whisking every 60 seconds, until it thickens—2 to 3 minutes more. Divide the custard among 10 dessert cups and put them into the refrigerator for at least 1 hour.

Just before serving, spread a dollop of yogurt over each custard and top it with the apricot purée.

# Mocha Pudding

**Serves 6**

Working time:
about 20
minutes

Total time:
about 1 hour
and 20
minutes

Calories
220
Protein
5g
Cholesterol
11mg
Total fat
7g
Saturated fat
4g
Sodium
110mg

| | | |
|---|---|---|
| **45 g** | plain chocolate | **$\frac{1}{2}$ oz** |
| **60 cl** | semi-skimmed milk | **1 pint** |
| **12.5 cl** | double-strength coffee | **4 fl oz** |
| **4 tbsp** | cornflour | **4 tbsp** |

| | | |
|---|---|---|
| **150 g** | caster sugar | **5 oz** |
| **$\frac{1}{8}$ tsp** | salt | **$\frac{1}{8}$ tsp** |
| **3 tbsp** | half cream, half milk | **3 tbsp** |

Place the chocolate in a 2 litre ($3\frac{1}{2}$ pint) glass bowl and cook it on medium (50 per cent power) for 2 to 3 minutes. (Though the chocolate will appear not to have melted, it will be soft.) Whisk the milk and coffee into the chocolate. Combine the cornflour, sugar and salt, and whisk them into the milk mixture. Microwave the contents of the bowl on high for 4 minutes. Whisk the mixture and continue cooking it on high, whisking every 60 seconds, until it thickens—4 to 6 minutes more. Pour the pudding into six dessert cups and refrigerate them for at least 1 hour.

Just before serving the pudding, dribble $\frac{1}{2}$ tablespoon of the cream-milk mixture over each portion.

# Cannelloni Stuffed with Turkey, Kale and Cheese

| | | |
|---|---|---|
| Serves 6 | | |
| Working time: about 30 minutes | | |
| Total time: about 2 hours | | |

| | | |
|---|---|---|
| Calories 450 | | |
| Protein 38g | | |
| Cholesterol 70mg | | |
| Total fat 12g | | |
| Saturated fat 7g | | |
| Sodium 470mg | | |

| | | | | | |
|---|---|---|---|---|---|
| 12 | cannelloni tubes (about 250 g/8 oz) | 12 | 250 g | low-fat cottage cheese | 8 oz |
| 500 g | turkey breast meat, cut into cubes | 1 lb | 6 tbsp | freshly grated Parmesan cheese | 6 tbsp |
| 1 | small onion, finely chopped | 1 | 250 g | kale, cooked and chopped | 8 oz |
| ½ tsp | fresh thyme | ½ tsp | | freshly ground black pepper | |
| 4 tbsp | dry vermouth | 4 tbsp | | grated nutmeg | |
| ½ litre | unsalted chicken stock | 16 fl oz | 30 g | unsalted butter | 1 oz |
| 250 g | low-fat ricotta cheese | 8 oz | 4 tbsp | plain flour | 4 tbsp |
| | | | ½ litre | skimmed milk | 16 fl oz |

Combine the turkey, onion, thyme and vermouth. Marinate for 30 minutes.

Strain the marinade into a large frying pan with the stock. Bring to a simmer. Add the turkey and poach until it is no longer pink— about 4 minutes. Lift the turkey into a food processor; reserve the poaching liquid. Process until finely chopped. Add the ricotta, cottage cheese, 4 tablespoons of Parmesan and the kale, and mix. Season with pepper and nutmeg; set aside.

Melt the butter in a large pan over medium heat. Whisk in the flour and cook for 2 minutes. Add the poaching liquid and bring to the boil, whisking. Pour in the milk and return to the boil, whisking. Simmer the sauce gently while you prepare the cannelloni.

Boil the cannelloni until *al dente*. Transfer to a bowl of cold water. Preheat the oven to 200°C (400°C or Mark 6). Drain and stuff with the turkey mixture.

Lay the cannelloni in a baking dish. Ladle on the sauce and sprinkle with the remaining Parmesan. Cover with foil and bake for 30 minutes. Remove the foil and brown the cannelloni under the grill. Serve.

# Lamb and Mushroom Burgers

Serves 4

Working time: about 30 minutes

Total time: about 1 hour and 5 minutes

Calories
350
Protein
36g
Cholesterol
80mg
Total fat
10g
Saturated fat
5g
Sodium
450mg

| | | |
|---|---|---|
| **500 g** | lean lamb (from the leg or loin), trimmed of fat minced | **1 lb** |
| **3 tbsp** | fresh granary or wholemeal breadcrumbs | **3 tbsp** |
| **2 tbsp** | fresh orange juice | **2 tbsp** |
| **¼ tsp** | finely grated lemon rind | **¼ tsp** |
| **1 tbsp** | chopped parsley | **1 tbsp** |
| **2 tsp** | finely cut chives | **2 tsp** |
| **⅛ tsp** | dried marjoram | **⅛ tsp** |
| **⅛ tsp** | salt | **⅛ tsp** |
| | freshly ground black pepper | |

| | | |
|---|---|---|
| **125 g** | button mushrooms, chopped | **4 oz** |
| **4** | granary baps, split in half | **4** |
| | carrot ribbons, for garnish | |
| | finely chopped celery, for garnish | |
| | shredded cabbage, for garnish | |
| | flat-leaf parsley, for garnish | |
| | **Mustard sauce** | |
| **1 tbsp** | grainy mustard | **1 tbsp** |
| **4 tbsp** | fromage frais | **4 tbsp** |
| **1 tbsp** | finely cut chives | **1 tbsp** |
| | freshly ground black pepper | |

Put the lamb, breadcrumbs, orange juice, lemon rind, parsley, chives, marjoram, salt and some pepper in a bowl and mix them thoroughly by hand. Set the bowl aside. Heat a heavy non-stick frying pan, brush it with oil, add the mushrooms and sauté them over high heat for 3 minutes, stirring them constantly. Allow the mushrooms to cool, then add them to the meat mixture. Shape the mixture into four burgers, each about 10 cm (4 inches) in diameter. Cover and refrigerate them for 30 minutes.

Meanwhile, combine the ingredients for the mustard sauce in a mixing bowl. Set the sauce aside.

Preheat the grill to hot, and cook the burgers for about 4 minutes on each side for medium meat. Toast the baps on the cut sides. Place each burger on the bottom half of a bap, garnish with the carrot, celery, cabbage and parsley, spoon on a portion of the mustard sauce and top with the other half of the bap.

# Meatballs with Lentils

Serves 6

Working time:
about 45
minutes

Total time:
about 1 hour
and 30
minutes

Calories
280
Protein
25g
Cholesterol
50mg
Total fat
8g
Saturated fat
3g
Sodium
205mg

| | | | | | | |
|---|---|---:|---|---|---|---:|
| 600 g | lean lamb (from the leg or loin), trimmed of fat and minced | 1¼ lb | 2 | carrots, chopped | | 2 |
| | | | 2 | sticks celery, chopped | | 2 |
| 4 tbsp | dry breadcrumbs | 4 tbsp | 250 g | fresh mushrooms, wiped clean and thinly sliced | | 8 oz |
| 2 tbsp | freshly grated Parmesan cheese | 2 tbsp | | | | |
| 1 tbsp | chopped, fresh rosemary, or 1 tsp dried rosemary, crumbled | 1 tbsp | 4 | garlic cloves, finely chopped | | 4 |
| | | | ½ tsp | hot red pepper flakes | | ½ tsp |
| 2 tsp | virgin olive oil | 2 tsp | 200 g | lentils, picked over | | 7 oz |
| 1 | turnip, chopped | 1 | ⅛ tsp | salt | | ⅛ tsp |
| 1 | onion, chopped | 1 | ¾ litre | unsalted chicken stock | | 1¼ pints |

Mix together the lamb, breadcrumbs, cheese and rosemary. With your hands, form the mixture into 12 balls. Heat the oil in a large, non-stick or heavy sauté pan set over high heat. Add the meatballs and brown them all over—4 to 5 minutes. Remove the meatballs from the pan with a slotted spoon and set them aside.

Add the turnip, onion, carrots, celery, mushrooms, garlic and red pepper flakes to the pan. Reduce the heat to low and sauté the vegetables until they are soft—about 8 minutes.

Increase the heat to medium high Add the lentils, salt and stock, and bring the liquid to the boil. Add the meatballs, cover the pan, leaving the lid slightly ajar, and reduce the heat. Simmer the meatballs and lentils until the lentils are tender—about 45 minutes.

Serve the meatballs and lentils piping hot.

# Tangerine Beef Stew

**Serves 4**

Working time:
about 40
minutes

Total time:
about 2 hours
and 30 minutes

Calories
595
Protein
29g
Cholesterol
70mg
Total fat
17g
Saturated fat
4g
Sodium
380mg

| | | | | | | |
|---|---|---|---|---|---|---|
| 3 tbsp | safflower oil | 3 tbsp | 3 | strips tangerine rind, each about | 3 |
| 500 g | stewing beef, trimmed and cut into cubes | 1 lb | | 5 cm (2 inches) long and 2.5 cm (1 inch) wide, pinned together with 1 whole clove | |
| ½ tbsp | Chinese five-spice powder | ½ tbsp | | | |
| 1 tbsp | flour | 1 tbsp | 250 g | fresh water chestnuts, peeled and sliced | 8 oz |
| 1 | garlic clove, finely chopped | 1 | | | |
| 2 tsp | finely chopped fresh ginger root | 2 tsp | 500 g | butternut squash cut into cubes | 1 lb |
| | | | ½ tsp | salt | ½ tsp |
| 2 | leeks, thinly sliced | 2 | 185 g | long-grain rice | 6½ oz |
| ¼ litre | red wine | 8 fl oz | 2 tbsp | julienned tangerine rind (optional), blanched | 2 tbsp |
| ½ litre | unsalted brown stock | 16 fl oz | | | |
| 4 tbsp | fresh tangerine juice | 4 tbsp | | | |

Pour 2 tablespoons of the oil into a heavy pan over medium-high heat. Coat the beef with five-spice powder and flour, then add it to the pan and brown all over. Lift it out onto a plate.

Clean the pan. Reduce the heat to low and pour in the remaining oil. Add the garlic, ginger and leeks, and cook, stirring, for 5 minutes. Return the beef cubes to the pan.

Add beef with the wine, stock, and tangerine rind and juice. Cover and simmer gently for 1½ hours.

Add the water chestnuts, squash and salt, and simmer until the squash is tender—about 20 minutes. Meanwhile, cook the rice. Spoon the stew over the rice; garnish, with the julienned rind.

# Rabbit Stew with Prunes

Serves 4

Working time: about 40 minutes

Total time: about 3 hours

Calories 355
Protein 30g
Cholesterol 60mg
Total fat 14g
Saturated fat 4g
Sodium 230mg

| | | | | | | |
|---|---|---|---|---|---|---|
| 1.25 kg | rabbit, cut into serving pieces | 2½ lb | 4 | garlic cloves, chopped | | 4 |
| ¼ litre | red wine | 8 fl oz | | freshly ground black pepper | | |
| 1 | bouquet garni, made | 1 | | flour for dredging (about 4 tbsp) | | |
| | by tying together 2 fresh | | 1 tbsp | safflower oil | 1 tbsp | |
| | thyme sprigs, several | | 15 g | unsalted butter | ½ oz | |
| | parsley stems and 1 bayleaf | | ¼ tsp | salt | ¼ tsp | |
| 1 | onion, chopped | 1 | ½ litre | unsalted chicken stock | 16 fl oz | |
| 1 | carrot, chopped | 1 | 175 g | stoned prunes | 6 oz | |

Marinate the rabbit for 2 hours at room temperature with the wine, bouquet garni, onion, carrot, garlic and some peppers. Remove the rabbit pieces from the marinade and pat them dry. Coat them lightly with the flour. Strain the marinade through a fine sieve, reserving the vegetables and the liquid separately.

Heat the oil and butter in a large, heavy pan over medium-high heat. Add the rabbit and sauté, sprinkling with the salt as it cooks, until browned. Transfer to a plate.

Add the reserved onion, garlic and carrot to the pan. Sauté, stirring constantly, until the onion is translucent—about 4 minutes. Pour in the strained marinade, then the stock; return the rabbit pieces to the pan. Bring to the boil, cover and reduce to a simmer; braise for 30 minutes.

Add the prunes and cover the pan; continue simmering until the rabbit is tender—about 20 minutes. With a slotted spoon, transfer the rabbit and prunes to a heated dish. Increase the heat to medium-high and reduce the sauce until thick enough to coat the back of a spoon—about 5 minutes. Pour the sauce over the rabbit and prunes, and serve with buttered noodles.

# Chicken Stew with Courgettes and Tomatoes

Serves 4

Working time: about 35 minutes

Total time: about one hour

Calories 325
Protein 32g
Cholesterol 65mg
Total fat 6g
Saturated fat 1g
Sodium 420mg

| | | |
|---|---|---|
| 1.25 kg | ripe tomatoes, skinned, seeded and chopped, or 800 g (28 oz) canned tomatoes, coarsely chopped, with their juice | 2½ lb |
| 35 cl | unsalted chicken stock | 12 fl oz |
| 1 tsp | sugar | 1 tsp |
| 2 | garlic cloves, finely chopped | 2 |
| 1 tsp | dried basil | 1 tsp |

| | | |
|---|---|---|
| ½ tsp | chili powder | ½ tsp |
| ½ tsp | salt | ½ tsp |
| | freshly ground black pepper | |
| 2 | chicken breasts, skinned | 2 |
| 90 g | wide egg noodles | 3 oz |
| 250 g | courgettes, trimmed and cut into thick rounds | 8 oz |

Put the tomatoes, stock, sugar, garlic, basil, chili powder, salt and some pepper into a large, heavy bottomed pan over medium heat. Bring the liquid to a simmer and cook the mixture for 10 minutes.

Add the chicken breasts to the pan and poach them for 12 minutes. With a slotted spoon, remove the slightly undercooked breasts and set them aside.

Cook the noodles in 1.5 litres (½ pints) of boiling water with ¾ teaspoon of salt for 3 minutes. Drain the noodles well, then add them to the stew along with the courgette rounds. When the chicken breasts are cool enough to handle, remove the meat from the bones. Cut the meat into 1 cm (½ inch) pieces and return it to the pan. Continue cooking the stew until the courgettes are tender—about 5 minutes more.

17

# Chicken Stew in Whole Green and Red Peppers

Serves 4

Working time: about 25 minutes

Total time: about 50 minutes

Calories 200
Protein 16g
Cholesterol 45mg
Total fat 11g
Saturated fat 2g
Sodium 330mg

| | | |
|---|---|---|
| 1½ tbsp | virgin olive oil | 1½ tbsp |
| 2 | large garlic cloves, finely chopped | 2 |
| 1 | onion, cut in half, the halves cut into pieces about 2.5 cm (1 inch) square | 1 |
| 4 | chicken thighs, skinned and boned, cut into chunks | 4 |
| 1 tbsp | dried oregano | 1 tbsp |
| | freshly ground black pepper | |

| | | |
|---|---|---|
| ½ tsp | salt | ½ tsp |
| 750 g | ripe tomatoes, skinned, seeded and coarsely chopped | 1½ lb |
| 3 | sweet green peppers, 1 cut into 2.5 cm (1 inch) squares | 3 |
| 3 | sweet red peppers, 1 cut into 2.5 cm (1 inch) squares | 3 |

Heat the oil in a large, heavy saucepan over medium-high heat. Add the garlic and onion and sauté, stirring, for 2 minutes. Add the chicken, oregano, pepper and salt, and sauté the chicken until golden-brown—about 5 minutes.

Reduce the heat and add the tomatoes with their juice to the pan. Then add the squares of green and red pepper. Cover the pan and simmer the stew until the chicken is tender and the peppers are soft—about 20 minutes. Add a little more water if necessary.

While the stew is simmering, cut the top off

each of the remaining peppers. Seed and derib them. Shave a thin slice from the bottom of each pepper so it will stand upright. Set a steamer in a saucepan and pour in enough water to barely reach the bottom of the steamer. Bring to the boil, put the peppers, including lids, in the steamer and tightly cover. Steam the peppers until they are tender—5 to 10 minutes.

Stand each steamed pepper in a small bowl. Spoon the stew into and around the peppers, and serve immediately.

# Beef Stew with Stout

Serves 6

Working time: about 40 minutes

Total time: about 2 hours and 15 minutes

Calories 260
Protein 27g
Cholesterol 75mg
Total fat 10g
Saturated fat 3g
Sodium 265mg

| | | | |
|---|---|---|---|
| 1½ tbsp | safflower oil | 1½ tbsp | |
| 750 g | lean stewing beef, trimmed and cut into cubes | 1½ lb | |
| 1 | large onion, chopped | 1 | |
| 250 g | button mushrooms, wiped clean, halved | 8 oz | |

| | | | |
|---|---|---|---|
| 2 tbsp | dark brown sugar | 2 tbsp | |
| ½ litre | unsalted brown or veal stock | 16 fl oz | |
| 35 cl | stout or dark beer | 12 fl oz | |
| ½ tsp | salt | ½ tsp | |
| | freshly ground black pepper | | |

Heat 1 tablespoon of the safflower oil in a large, heavy frying pan over medium-high heat. Add the beef cubes and sauté them, turning them frequently, until they are browned all over—about 8 minutes. Using a slotted spoon, transfer the beef to a heavy-bottomed saucepan.

Add the remaining oil to the frying pan along with the onion, mushrooms and brown sugar. Sauté the mixture, stirring frequently, until the mushrooms begin to brown and their liquid has evaporated—about 10 minutes. Transfer the onion-mushroom mixture to the saucepan, then add the stock, the stout or dark beer, the salt and some pepper.

Reduce the heat to very low, cover the saucepan, and gently simmer the stew until the beef is tender—1½ to 2 hours.

# Pork and Apple Stew

Serves 4

Working time: about 30 minutes

Total time: about 1 hour and 45 minutes

Calories 280
Protein 24g
Cholesterol 70mg
Total fat 12g
Saturated fat 2g
Sodium 265mg

| | | | | | |
|---|---|---|---|---|---|
| 2 tbsp | safflower oil | 2 tbsp | 1 | onion, sliced | 1 |
| 500 g | boneless pork shoulder, fat trimmed away, cut into 5 cm (1 inch) chunks | 1 lb | 1 tsp | dried sage | 1 tsp |
| | | | ¼ tsp | salt | ¼ tsp |
| 3 | cooking apples, 2 cut into large chunks, 1 cored and thinly sliced | 3 | | freshly ground black pepper | |
| | | | ¾ litre | unsalted brown stock | 1¼ pints |
| | | | 1 | ripe tomato, skinned, seeded and chopped | 1 |

Heat 1 tablespoon of the oil in a heavy-bottomed pan over medium-high heat. Add the pork and onion, and sauté them until the pork is lightly browned and the onion is translucent—about 5 minutes. Add the apple chunks, sage, salt, a generous grinding of pepper and the stock. Reduce the heat to maintain a simmer, then cover the pan and cook the stew until the pork is tender—about 1 hour.

Remove the pork from the pan and set it aside. Carefully skim as much fat from the surface of the liquid as you can. Purée the apple chunks and onion with their cooking liquid in several batches in a food mill. (Alternatively, purée the mixture in a food processor, then press the purée through a fine sieve with a wooden spoon.) Return the purée and the pork to the pan, and heat the stew over medium-high heat.

While the stew is heating, pour the remaining safflower oil into a heavy frying pan over medium-high heat. Add the uncooked apple slices and sauté them until they are lightly browned. Stir them into the stew with the tomatoes and serve at once.

# Cod Stewed with Onions, Potatoes, Sweetcorn and Tomatoes

Working time: about 15 minutes

Total time: about 1 hour

Calories 310
Protein 19g
Cholesterol 30mg
Total fat 4g
Saturated fat 1g
Sodium 305mg

| | | |
|---|---|---|
| 1 tbsp | virgin olive oil | 1 tbsp |
| 500 g | onions, thinly sliced | 1 lb |
| 1 kg | waxy potatoes, peeled and thinly sliced | 2 lb |
| 500 g | fresh or frozen sweetcorn kernels | 1 lb |
| $\frac{1}{2}$ | green pepper, seeded, deribbed and diced | $\frac{1}{2}$ |
| | Tabasco sauce | |

| | | |
|---|---|---|
| 500 g | cod (or haddock), skinned, rinsed, cut into chunks | 1 lb |
| 1.25 kg | ripe tomatoes, skinned, seeded and chopped, or 800 g (28 oz) canned whole tomatoes drained and chopped | $2\frac{1}{2}$ lb |
| $\frac{1}{4}$ tsp | salt | $\frac{1}{4}$ tsp |
| | freshly ground black pepper | |
| | fresh coriander leaves for garnish | |

In a large, heavy-bottomed pan, heat the oil over medium heat. Add a layer of onions and a layer of potatoes. Sprinkle some of the sweetcorn and green pepper on top. Dribble a few drops of Tabasco sauce over the vegetables. Add a layer of fish and tomatoes and season with all of the salt and some pepper. Repeat the process, build up successive layers, until the remaining vegetables and fish are used. Cover the pan and cook over medium-low heat till the potatoes are done—about 45 minutes. Garnish the stew with the coriander leaves if you are using them. Serve at once.

21

# Oxtails Braised with Carrots

Serves 4

Working time:
about 35
minutes

Total time:
about 3 hours

Calories
295
Protein
32g
Cholesterol
75mg
Total fat
9g
Saturated fat
3g
Sodium
245mg

| | | |
|---|---|---|
| 1 tbsp | safflower oil | 1 tbsp |
| 1 | bunch spring onions, trimmed and chopped | 1 |
| 1½ tbsp | finely chopped fresh ginger root | 1½ tbsp |
| 2 | garlic cloves, finely chopped | 2 |
| ½ litre | unsalted brown stock | 16 fl oz |
| ¼ litre | dry sherry | 8 fl oz |
| 2 tsp | fermented black beans, crushed | 2 tsp |
| 1 tsp | chili sauce | 1 tsp |
| 2 tsp | hoisin sauce | 2 tsp |
| 1.5 kg | oxtails, trimmed of all fat and blanched in boiling water for 3 minutes | 3 lb |
| 5 | carrots, roll-cut | 5 |
| 175 g | fresh Asian wheat noodles | 6 oz |

In a heavy pan large enough to hold the oxtails in a single layer, heat the oil over medium-high heat. Add the spring onions, ginger and garlic, and sauté them for 2 minutes. Pour in the stock, ½ litre (16 fl oz) of water and the sherry, then stir in the crushed black beans, chili sauce and hoisin sauce. Add the oxtails. Bring the liquid to the boil, then reduce the heat to very low and cook the oxtails, covered, for 1 hour. Turn the oxtails over and cook them until they are very tender —about 1½ hours more.

Add the carrots and simmer them until they are just tender—15 to 20 minutes.

Pour the stew into a colander set over a large bowl. Remove the oxtail meat from the bones and return it to the pan along with the carrots and other solids. Degrease the liquid, then pour it back into the pan. Reheat the stew over medium heat.

Add the noodles to 2 litres (3½ pints) of boiling water with 1 teaspoon of salt. Start testing the noodles after 3 minutes and cook them until they are *al dente*. Drain the noodles, then divide them between six soup bowls. Top the noodles with the oxtails and carrots, ladle some liquid over all and serve immediately.

# Pork Carbonnade

**Serves 8**

Working time:
about 40
minutes

Total time:
about 2 hours
and 20
minutes

Calories
480
Protein
38g
Cholesterol
70mg
Total fat
25g
Saturated fat
6g
Sodium
550mg

| | | |
|---|---|---|
| 1 kg | lean pork shoulder, cubed | 2 lb |
| 4 tbsp | plain wholemeal flour | 4 tbsp |
| 60 g | polyunsaturated margarine | 2 oz |
| 3 tbsp | safflower oil | 3 tbsp |
| 3 | large onions, halved and sliced | 3 |
| 3 | garlic cloves, crushed | 3 |
| 45 cl | unsalted chicken stock | $\frac{3}{4}$ pint |
| 45 cl | light ale | $\frac{3}{4}$ pint |
| 3 tsp | wine vinegar | 3 tsp |
| 1 tsp | salt | 1 tsp |
| | freshly ground black pepper | |
| 1 | bouquet garni | 1 |
| 8 | slices French bread, 1 cm | 8 |
| | ($\frac{1}{2}$ inch) thick | |
| 1$\frac{1}{2}$ tbsp | grainy mustard | 1$\frac{1}{2}$ tbsp |
| 3 tbsp | chopped parsley | 3 tbsp |
| 90 g | grated Cheddar cheese | 3 oz |
| | fresh bay leaves, for garnish | |

Preheat the oven to 180°C (350°F or Mark 4). Coat the pork in the flour. Heat half of the margarine with the oil in a large pan and gently cook the onions and two garlic cloves for 3 minutes.

Lift the onions out into a casserole. Add the pork to the pan, reserving excess flour. Fry over high heat until sealed all over; add the remaining flour and cook for 1 minute. Stir in the stock and ale and bring almost to the boil, stirring. Add the vinegar and seasoning, pour over the onions, then add the bouquet garni.

Cover and cook in the oven for 1$\frac{1}{2}$ hours.

Meanwhile, toast the bread on one side. Mix the remaining margarine, the mustard, 2 tablespoons parsley and remaining garlic. Spread over the untoasted sides.

When the casserole is cooked, remove the bouquet garni. Arrange the bread, toasted sides down, on top. Sprinkle with cheddar cheese, then cook, uncovered, for 25 minutes more until golden. Garnish with parsley and bay leaves and serve.

# Red Pepper Pork with Mint

| | | |
|---|---|---|
| Serves 4 | | Calories 220 |
| Working (and total) time: about 35 minutes | | Protein 24g |
| | | Cholesterol 70mg |
| | | Total fat 12g |
| | | Saturated fat 3g |
| | | Sodium 90mg |

| | | |
|---|---|---|
| 500 g | pork fillet or loin, trimmed of fat and thinly sliced | 1 lb |
| 1 tbsp | virgin olive oil | 1 tbsp |
| 2 | sweet red peppers, thinly sliced | 2 |
| | freshly ground black pepper | |

| | | |
|---|---|---|
| 500 g | tomatoes, skinned, seeded and chopped | 1 lb |
| ¼ tsp | salt | ¼ tsp |
| 2 tbsp | finely chopped fresh mint | 2 tbsp |
| 45 g | fromage frais (optional) | 1½ oz |

Heat the oil in a heavy frying pan; add the red peppers and sauté for 1 minute. Add the pork slices and brown them over high heat. Season with some black pepper, then cover the pan and reduce the heat to low. After 5 minutes, add the tomatoes; continue to cook, covered, for 10 to 15 minutes, or until the meat is tender and the tomato-pepper mixture is well reduced. Season with the salt and some more pepper, if required.

Remove the pan from the heat and leave it to cool for 1 minute, then stir in the mint and, if you are using it, the *fromage frais*. Serve at once.

# Stuffed Leeks with a Gruyère Sauce

Serves 4

Working time: about 1 hour

Total time: about 1 hour 30 minutes

Calories 250
Protein 10g
Cholesterol 25mg
Total fat 9g
Saturated fat 3g
Sodium 330mg

| | | |
|---|---|---|
| 600 g | leeks, trimmed, washed cut to 10 cm (4 inch) lengths | 1¼ lb |
| 125 g | buckwheat, cooked in ½ litre (16 fl oz) vegetable stock | 4 oz |
| 15 g | unsalted butter | ½ oz |
| 150 g | finely diced mushrooms | 6 oz |

| | | |
|---|---|---|
| 125 g | sweet red pepper, chopped | 4 oz |
| ¼ tsp | salt | ¼ tsp |
| 2 tbsp | fresh breadcrumbs | 2 tbsp |
| | **Gruyère Sauce** | |
| 250 g | low-fat fromage frais | 8 oz |
| 60 g | Gruyère cheese, grated | 2 oz |
| ⅛ tsp | grated nutmeg | ⅛ tsp |

Separate 26 outer leaves from the leeks. Blanch in boiling water for 1 minute, refresh under cold water and dry flat on paper towels. Finely chop the insides of the leeks. Sauté them in half of the butter with the mushrooms. Remove from the heat. Stir in the sweet pepper and cooked buckwheat; season with salt.

Preheat the oven to 200°C (400°F or Mark 6). Divide the buckwheat mixture into 12. Cut 2 of the blanched leek leaves into 6 ribbons each. Fashion 12 rolls round the stuffing with the remaining leaves and tie with ribbons. Lay the rolls in a gratin dish.

Blend together the sauce ingredients and pour over the ends of the leeks. Brush the middles with a little melted butter. Place the gratin dish in a roasting pan with water coming ⅔ of the way up the sides of the dish. Cover the gratin dish with foil and bake for 25 minutes.

Preheat the grill. Remove the gratin dish from the oven and discard the foil. Sprinkle the breadcrumbs over the sauce, cover the middle of the leeks with foil, and grill for 5 to 7 minutes.

Serve with sliced, sautéed mushrooms if desired.

# Spiced Red Cabbage

Serves 6

Working time:
about 20
minutes

Total time:
about 1 hour
and 50
minutes

Calories
330

Protein
15g

Cholesterol
20mg

Total fat
13g

Saturated fat
4g

Sodium
390mg

| 1 tbsp | juniper berries | 1 tbsp | 30 cl | dry cider | ½ pint |
| 1 tbsp | coriander seeds | 1 tbsp | | freshly ground black pepper | |
| 2 tbsp | virgin olive oil | 2 tbsp | 3 | large green cooking apples | 3 |
| 5 | garlic cloves, sliced | 5 | | (750 g/1½ lb), cored, peeled, halved | |
| 1 | large red cabbage (about 2.25 kg/ | 1 | | and placed in acidulated water | |
| | 1½ lb), trimmed and sliced | | 90 g | Edam cheese thinly sliced | 3 oz |

Preheat the oven to 180°C (350°F or Mark 4). Crush the juniper berries and coriander seeds using a mortar and pestle.

Heat the oil over medium heat in a 7 litre (12 pint) fireproof casserole. Add the garlic and crushed spices and stir-fry them briefly, then add the red cabbage and stir-fry for 3 to 4 minutes. Remove the casserole from the heat. Pour the cider over the cabbage and season it with black pepper. Cover the casserole and cook the cabbage in the oven for 1 hour.

Stir the cabbage and transfer it to a 3.5 litre

(6 pint) ovenproof casserole—the cabbage will have halved in volume by this stage. Drain the apple halves, pat them dry on paper towels and lay them on top of the cabbage. Cover the casserole and return the cabbage to the oven for a further 30 minutes.

Preheat the grill to medium. Remove the casserole from the oven, take off the lid and, without stirring the contents, lay the slices of cheese over the apples. Put the casserole under the grill for about 5 minutes, until the cheese has melted and begun to brown. Serve the cabbage at once.

# Provençal Casserole

**Serves 6**

**Working time:**
about 30 minutes

**Total time:**
about 3 hours (includes soaking)

**Calories**
180
**Protein**
11g
**Cholesterol**
0mg
**Total fat**
3g
**Saturated fat**
1g
**Sodium**
90mg

| | | |
|---|---|---|
| **250 g** | dried flageolet beans, picked over | **8 oz** |
| **1 tbsp** | virgin olive oil | **1 tbsp** |
| **15 cl** | unsalted vegetable stock | **¼ pint** |
| **1** | large onion, sliced | **1** |
| **1** | garlic clove, crushed | **1** |
| **1** | sweet red pepper, seeded, deribbed and sliced | **1** |
| **500 g** | courgettes, thickly sliced | **1 lb** |
| **1** | aubergine, cut into large dice | **1** |

| | | |
|---|---|---|
| **500 g** | tomatoes, skinned, seeded and roughly chopped, or 300 g (10 oz) canned tomatoes, drained and roughly chopped | **1 lb** |
| **725 g** | button mushrooms, wiped clean, stems trimmed | **4 oz** |
| **2 tsp** | chopped fresh oregano, or ½ tsp dried oregano | **2 tsp** |
| **¼ tsp** | freshly ground black pepper | **¼ tsp** |
| **¼ tsp** | salt | **¼ tsp** |

Rinse the beans under cold running water, boil them, well covered with water for 2 minutes then leave to soak for at least 1 hour.

Rinse the beans, place them in a clean pan, cover well with water and boil for 10 minutes, then drain and rinse them again. Wash out the pan, replace the beans, cover them well with water and bring it to the boil. Reduce to a strong simmer, and cook, covered, until they are tender—about 1 hour. Add more water if necessary. Drain and rinse the cooked beans in a colander.

Heat the oil in a large, fireproof casserole and cook the onion and garlic gently for a few minutes, until softened but not browned. Add the red pepper, courgettes, aubergine and tomatoes, and cook over medium-low for 1 to 2 minutes, stirring. Reduce the heat and add the mushrooms, beans, stock, oregano, black pepper and salt. Mix well, cover, and simmer over gently, stirring occasionally, for 25 minutes, or until the vegetables are tender. Serve hot.

# Vegetable Lasagne

**Serves 6**

**Working time: about 1 hour and 30 minutes**

**Total time: about 2 hours and 15 minutes**

Calories 295
Protein 13g
Cholesterol 55mg
Total fat 12g
Saturated fat 5g
Sodium 280mg

| | | |
|---|---|---|
| **18** | sheets 'no pre-cook' lasagne | **18** |
| **1 tbsp** | virgin olive oil | **1 tbsp** |
| **1** | onion, finely chopped | **1** |
| **1** | leek, trimmed, washed and sliced | **1** |
| **2** | garlic cloves, crushed | **2** |
| **175 g** | broccoli florets | **6 oz** |
| **125 g** | French beans, topped and tailed, cut into short lengths | **4 oz** |
| **6** | sticks celery, thinly sliced | **6** |
| **1** | yellow pepper, thinly sliced | **1** |
| **1 tsp** | mixed dried herbs | **1 tsp** |
| **1 tbsp** | chopped parsley | **1 tbsp** |

| | | |
|---|---|---|
| **400 g** | canned tomatoes, sieved | **14 oz** |
| **¼ tsp** | salt | **¼ tsp** |
| | freshly ground black pepper | |
| **30 g** | Parmesan cheese, grated | **1 oz** |
| | **Nutmeg sauce** | |
| **30 g** | unsalted butter | **1 oz** |
| **30 g** | plain flour | **1 oz** |
| **30 cl** | skimmed milk | **½ pint** |
| **½ tsp** | freshly grated nutmeg | **½ tsp** |
| **⅛ tsp** | salt | **⅛ tsp** |
| | freshly ground black pepper | |

Sauté the onion and leek in the oil until softened. Stir in the garlic, all the vegetables and herbs, the sieved tomatoes and seasoning. Boil, then, simmer, partially covered, until the vegetables are tender and the liquid has thickened.

Preheat the oven to 200°C (400°F or Mark 6).

Grease a large ovenproof dish and line the bottom with six sheets of lasagne. Pour in half of the vegetable filling then cover with six more sheets. Pour in the rest of the vegetables and place the remaining sheets over the top.

To make the sauce, melt the butter in a saucepan over medium heat. Add the flour, then stir in the milk. Bring to the boil, stirring until it thickens. Stir in the nutmeg and seasoning. Reduce the heat to low and simmer the sauce for 5 minutes, stirring frequently. Pour the sauce over the top and spread it to cover the entire surface. Sprinkle the Parmesan over the sauce. Cook the lasagne in the oven for 40 minutes, until golden-brown and bubbling hot.

# Salad-Filled Potato Pie

**Serves 6**

Working time: about 30 minutes

Total time: about 40 minutes

Calories 190
Protein 5g
Cholesterol 45mg
Total fat 4g
Saturated fat 1g
Sodium 230mg

| | | |
|---|---|---|
| **1 kg** | large potatoes, scrubbed | **2 lb** |
| **1 tbsp** | potato flour | **1 tbsp** |
| **2 tbsp** | skimmed mllk | **2 tbsp** |
| **3 cl** | plain low-fat yogurt | **1 fl oz** |
| **45 g** | crème fraîche | **1½ oz** |
| **2 tbsp** | finely chopped fresh dill | **2 tbsp** |
| **¾ tsp** | salt | **¾ tsp** |
| | freshly grated nutmeg | |

| | | |
|---|---|---|
| **1 tsp** | safflower oil | **1 tsp** |
| **60 g** | watercress leaves | **2 oz** |
| **100 g** | cucumber, peeled and cut into long bâtonnets | **3½ oz** |
| **200 g** | tomatoes, skinned, seeded and chopped | **7 oz** |
| | freshly ground black pepper | |
| **½ tsp** | mild paprika | **½ tsp** |

Prick the potatoes all over with a fork and arrange in a circle, on a double layer of paper towels, in the microwave. Microwave on high for 12 to 15 minutes, rotating every 3 minutes, until cooked through. Leave to rest for a further 3 minutes, then peel and mash them.

Blend the potato flour with the milk, then beat in the egg, yogurt, *crème fraîche*, dill, ½ teaspoon of the salt and some grated nutmeg. Beat into the mashed potato.

Brush a 25 by 16 cm (10 by 6 inch) baking dish with the oil. Spread half of the potato mixture over the base and sides. Scatter the watercress over the potato to within 1 cm (½ inch) of the sides. Arrange the cucumber and tomatoes on top. Sprinkle the filling with the remaining salt and plenty of black pepper.

Spread the remaining potato over the filling. Mark the surface with a fork and sift the paprika over the top.

Cover the dish with plastic film, leaving two corners open. Microwave on high for 7 to 10 minutes, giving a quarter turn every 2 minutes, until heated through. Remove from the oven and allow to rest for a further 3 minutes. Serve.

# Roast Sirloin of Beef with Yorkshire Pudding

Serves 6

Working time: about 30 minutes

Total time: about 1 hours 35 minutes

Calories 345
Protein 40g
Cholesterol 115mg
Total fat 15g
Saturated fat 5g
Sodium 133mg

| | | |
|---|---|---|
| 1 kg | beef sirloin, boned, trimmed, rolled and tied | 2-2¼ lb |
| 1 tbsp | grated fresh horseradish | 1 tbsp |
| 2 tsp | grainy mustard | 2 tsp |
| 4 tsp | plain flour | 4 tsp |
| 30 cl | brown stock | ½ pint |

| Yorkshire puddings | | |
|---|---|---|
| 60 g | plain flour | 2 oz |
| ⅛ tsp | salt | ⅛ tsp |
| | freshly ground black pepper | |
| 1 | egg, beaten | 1 |
| 12.5 cl | semi-skimmed milk | 4 fl oz |
| 1½ tbsp | virgin olive oil | 1½ tbsp |

Preheat the oven to 190°C (375°F or Mark 5). Brush the joint with horseradish and mustard. Dust a roasting bag with 1 teaspoon of the flour, then place the joint in the bag. Seal, leaving an opening for steam.

Place the bag in a roasting pan, opening uppermost. Allow 15 minutes roasting time per 500 g (1 lb) for rare meat, 20 minutes for medium and 25 minutes for well done.

Sift the flour and seasoning into a bowl, make a well in the centre and add the egg. Make up the milk to 15 cl (¼ pint) with cold water, then whisk it into the flour and egg. Beat well. Cover and set aside.

Remove the joint from the oven but leave it in the bag. Increase the oven temperature to 220°C (425°F or Mark 7). Brush 12 patty tins with oil and place in the hottest part of the oven until smoking hot. Remove from the oven, whisk the batter and pour it into the tins. Return to the oven and cook until golden and well risen.

While the Yorkshire puddings are cooking, remove the joint from the bag and keep warm. Pour the cooking juices into a saucepan, add the stock and bring to the boil. Mix the remaining flour with 1 tablespoon of cold water, add a little hot stock, then stir into the pan. Simmer, stirring, to reduce and thicken. Serve with beef and Yorkshire puddings.

# Pot Roast with Parsnips

**Serves 10**

Working time: about 30 minutes

Total time: about 2 hours 30 minutes

Calories 290
Protein 33g
Cholesterol 95mg
Total fat 10g
Saturated fat 3g
Sodium 215mg

| | | | | | | |
|---|---|---|---|---|---|---|
| 1.75 kg | beef topside, trimmed | 3½ lb | 1 tbsp | chopped fresh thyme | 1 tbsp |
| 1 tbsp | safflower oil | 1 tbsp | 3 | carrots peeled and cut on the diagonal | 3 |
| ¼ litre | unsalted brown or chicken stock | 8 fl oz | 350 g | celeriac, peeled and cut into cubes | 12 oz |
| 400 g | canned tomatoes, puréed and strained | 14 oz | 5 | small onions, peeled and halved crosswise | 5 |
| 2 | garlic cloves, finely chopped | 2 | 500 g | parsnips or turnips, peeled and cut into 1 cm (½ inch) pieces | 1 lb |
| ½ tsp | salt | ½ tsp | | | |
| 10 | black peppercorns, crushed | 10 | | | |
| 1 | bay leaf | 1 | | | |

Heat the oil in a large fireproof casserole over medium-high heat. Add the joint and brown it on both sides—1 to 2 minutes per side—then pour in the stock and enough water to cover the meat. Add the puréed tomatoes, the garlic, salt, peppercorns, bay leaf and thyme, and bring the liquid to the boil. Reduce the heat to low, cover the casserole, and simmer the beef until it feels very tender when pierced with a fork—2 to 3 hours. Remove the pot roast from the casserole without discarding the cooking liquid; keep the roast warm.

Add the carrots, the celeriac, the onions, and the parsnips or turnips to the cooking liquid. Simmer the vegetables until they are tender—approximately 20 minutes.

Slice the roast and arrange it on a serving platter. Surround the meat with the vegetables. Spoon some of the cooking liquid over the meat and pour the rest into a sauce bowl to be passed separately.

# Beef and Potato Pie

Serves 4

Working time:
about 1 hour

Total time:
about 2 hours

Calories
485
Protein
32g
Cholesterol
70mg
Total fat
12g
Saturated fat
3g
Sodium
270mg

| | | |
|---|---|---|
| ι00 g | topside of beef, trimmed of fat and minced | 1 ¼ lb |
| 1 kg | potatoes, peeled and quartered | 2 lb |
| 2 tbsp | skimmed milk | 2 tbsp |
| 2 tbsp | chopped parsley | 2 tbsp |
| ¼ tsp | salt | ¼ tsp |
| 4 tsp | safflower oil | 4 tsp |
| 3 tbsp | plain flour | 3 tbsp |

| | | |
|---|---|---|
| ½ litre | unsalted brown or chicken stock | 16 fl oz |
| 125 g | shallots, thinly sliced | 4 oz |
| 90 g | dried apples, chopped | 3 oz |
| 2 tbsp | cider vinegar | 2 tbsp |
| 1 tbsp | fresh thyme, or 1 tsp dried thyme | 1 tbsp |
| | freshly ground black pepper | |

Preheat the oven to 230°C (450°F or Mark 8). Boil the potatoes until tender—15 to 20 minutes. Drain the potatoes, spread them out on a baking sheet, and place them in the oven to dry. After 5 minutes, remove them from the oven and purée through a sieve set over a bowl. Combine with the milk, parsley and salt and set them aside.

Blend 2 teaspoons of the oil and the flour in a saucepan over low heat and cook for 1 minute. Whisk in the stock and simmer gently until it thickens—about 2 minutes. Remove from the heat.

Place the shallots, apples and vinegar in a heavy, frying pan and cook over medium heat until the vinegar has evaporated and the shallots are limp—about 2 minutes. Add the beef and brown it over high heat. Remove the pan from the heat and stir in the thyme, some pepper and the thickened stock.

Divide the meat mixture evenly between four small gratin dishes. Top the meat with the potato mixture, smooth the surface with a spatula, and flute the potatoes using the edge of the spatula. Brush the surface with the remaining 2 teaspoons of oil. Bake the beef and potatoe pie until it lightly browns—20 to 30 minutes.

# Beetroot Beefburgers

Serves 8
Working time:
about 20
minutes
Total time:
about 2 hours

Calories
320
Protein
31g
Cholesterol
70mg
Total fat
10g
Saturated fat
3g
Sodium
310mg

| | | | | | | |
|---|---|---|---|---|---|---|
| 1.25 kg | topside of beef, trimmed of fat and minced | 2½ lb | 4 tbsp | dry breadcrumbs | 4 tbsp |
| 1 kg | beetroots, washed, all but 2.5 cm (1 inch) of the stems cut off | 2 lb | 4 tbsp | distilled white vinegar freshly ground black pepper | 4 tbsp |
| 1 | small onion, peeled and grated | 1 | 2 tsp | safflower oil | 2 tsp |
| 8 | cornichons, chopped, or 2 small gherkins, chopped | 8 | 12.5 cl | unsalted brown or chicken stock | 4 fl oz |
| | | | 1 tsp | caraway seeds | 1 tsp |
| | | | 8 | hamburger buns or baps, split | 8 |

Preheat the oven to 200°C (400°F or Mark 6). Wrap all the beetroots together in a single package of aluminium foil and bake them until they are tender—approximately 1 hour. Unwrap them and let them cool. Peel and grate the beetroots. Put 90 g (3 oz) of the beetroot into a bowl, and set the remainder aside.

Add the minced beef, onion, cornichons or gherkins, breadcrumbs, vinegar and some pepper to the bowl. Mix the ingredients thoroughly, then shape the mixture into eight patties.

Heat the oil in a large, non-stick frying pan over medium-high heat. Add the patties to the pan and brown them for about 1 minute per side. Add the reserved beetroot, the stock, caraway seeds and some pepper. Cover the pan and reduce the heat to medium low. Simmer the mixture for 20 minutes.

Serve the beefburgers in the buns or baps, with the beetroot alongside.

# Minced Beef with Sweet Peppers and Pasta

Serves 6

Working (and total) time: about 30 minutes

Calories 415
Protein 28g
Cholesterol 50mg
Total fat 9g
Saturated fat 3g
Sodium 260mg

| | | |
|---|---|---|
| 600 g | topside of beef, trimmed and minced | 1¼ lb |
| 2 | sweet red peppers | 2 |
| 1 tbsp | olive oil | 1 tbsp |
| 2 | onions, finely chopped | 2 |
| 1 tsp | fennel seeds | 1 tsp |
| 6 | garlic cloves, thinly sliced | 6 |
| ¼ tsp | salt | ¼ tsp |
| | freshly ground black pepper | |
| 400 g | canned tomatoes, chopped, with their juice | 14 oz |

| | | |
|---|---|---|
| 6 tbsp | red wine vinegar | 6 tbsp |
| 1 tsp | sugar | 1 tsp |
| 350 g | courgettes, trimmed, halved lengthwise and cut on the diagonal into 5 mm (¼ inch) pieces | 12 oz |
| 350 g | penne or other tubular pasta | 12 oz |
| ¼ litre | unsalted chicken stock | 8 fl oz |
| 30 g | fresh basil, shredded | 1 oz |
| 4 tbsp | freshly grated Parmesan cheese | 4 tbsp |

Grill the peppers until their skins blister. Transfer to a bowl and cover it with plastic film to loosen the skins. When cool, peel and seed them, over a bowl to catch any juice. Cut into thin strips and strain the juice.

Heat the oil in a heavy frying pan over medium-high heat. Add the beef, onions, fennel seeds, garlic and seasoning. Cook, stirring, until the beef browns. Add the chopped tomatoes and their juice, the vinegar and the sugar. Reduce the heat and simmer the mixture for 10 minutes. Add the courgettes and the peppers and juice; cook the mixture for another 5 minutes.

Meanwhile, cook the pasta for 6 minutes in salted boiling water. Drain and return it to the pan; pour in the stock, cover, and bring to a simmer. Cook the pasta 1 minute longer, then add the beef mixture, basil and plenty of pepper, and stir. Simmer, stirring, until most of the liquid is absorbed.

Transfer to a large bowl. Sprinkle on the Parmesan, and serve.

# Lettuce Leaves in a Garlicky Vinaigrette

Serves 6 as a
first course or
side dish

Working time:
about 10
minutes

Total time:
about 25
minutes

Calories
110
Protein
3g
Cholesterol
0mg
Total fat
5g
Saturated fat
1g
Sodium
150mg

| | | | |
|---|---|---|---|
| **1** | whole garlic bulb, the cloves separated and peeled | **1 tbsp** | safflower oil | **1 tbsp** |
| **1 tbsp** | balsamic vinegar, or $\frac{3}{4}$ tbsp red wine vinegar mixed with $\frac{1}{4}$ tsp honey | **1 tbsp** | $\frac{1}{8}$ **tsp** | salt | $\frac{1}{8}$ **tsp** |
| **1 tbsp** | virgin olive oil | **1 tbsp** | | freshly ground black pepper | |
| | | | **2** | large round lettuces, leaves washed and dried | **2** |
| | | | **12** | thin French bread slices, toasted | **12** |

Put the garlic cloves into a small saucepan and pour in enough water to cover them. Bring the liquid to the boil, then reduce the heat, and simmer the garlic until it is quite tender—about 15 minutes. Increase the heat and boil the liquid until only about 2 tablespoons remain—2 to 3 minutes.

Pour the contents of the saucepan into a sieve set over a small bowl. With a wooden spoon, mash the garlic through the sieve into the bowl. Whisk the vinegar into the garlic mixture, then incorporate the olive oil, safflower oil, salt and some pepper.

Toss the lettuce leaves with the dressing; garnish the salad with the toast and serve at once.

# Spirals with Spring Vegetables

| | | |
|---|---|---|
| Serves 8 as a first course | | |
| Working time: about 40 minutes | | |
| Total time: about 1 hour | | |

| | | |
|---|---|---|
| Calories 170 | | |
| Protein 5g | | |
| Cholesterol 0mg | | |
| Total fat 4g | | |
| Saturated fat 1g | | |
| Sodium 175mg | | |

| | | | | | |
|---|---|---|---|---|---|
| ¼ litre | unsalted chicken | 8 fl oz | 3 | carrots | 3 |
| 250 g | fresh shiitake mushrooms cut into pieces | 8 oz | 2 tbsp | fresh lemon juice | 2 tbsp |
| 1 | large onion | 1 | 250 g | asparagus, sliced into 2.5 cm (1 inch) lengths | 8 oz |
| ½ tsp | salt | ½ tsp | 250 g | pasta spirals or other fancy pasta | 8 oz |
| 2 tbsp | virgin olive oil | 2 tbsp | 4 tbsp | thinly sliced fresh basil leaves | 4 tbsp |
| 4 tbsp | red wine vinegar | 4 tbsp | 4 tbsp | freshly ground black pepper | 4 tbsp |

Cook the mushrooms and onions in 17.5 cl (6 fl oz) of the stock with ¼ teaspoon salt, until the stock evaporates. Stir in 1 tablespoon of olive oil and cook for 3 minutes more. Transfer to a large bowl and return the pan to the stove over low heat. Pour in the vinegar and remaining stock. Simmer, stirring, until only 2 tablespoons of liquid remain. Stir the reduced liquid into the mushrooms and onions.

Bring 2 litres (3½ pints) of water to the boil. While the water heats, roll cut the carrots.

Add to the water 1 tablespoon of the lemon juice, ¼ teaspoon of salt and the roll-cut carrots. Boil for about 6 minutes. Add the asparagus pieces and boil them for 30 seconds. Transfer the vegetables to a colander; reserve the cooking liquid. Refresh the vegetables under cold water; when thoroughly cooled, drain, and toss them with the mushrooms and onions. Refrigerate.

Return the water to a boil; add the pasta and remaining lemon juice. Cook until the pasta is *al dente*. Drain the pasta and rinse. Add it to the vegetables with the remaining oil, the basil, salt and plenty of pepper. Toss well and chill for 10 minutes before serving.

# Red, White and Green Salad

Serves 6 as a
first course or
side dish

Working time:
about 20
minutes

Total time:
about 1 hour

Calories
60
Protein
2g
Cholesterol
0mg
Total fat
4g
Saturated fat
0g
Sodium
75mg

| 250 g | beetroot, rinsed | 8 oz | 1 | head of radicchio cut into chiffonade | 1 |
| 3 tbsp | raspberry vinegar | 3 tbsp | 1 | large head of chicory, cored, | 1 |
| | or red wine vinegar | | | cut in half crosswise, | |
| 2 tsp | Dijon mustard | 2 tsp | | the halves julienned | |
| 2 tsp | grainy mustard | 2 tsp | 125 g | lamb's lettuce (corn salad or | 4 oz |
| ¼ tsp | honey | ¼ tsp | | mâche), washed and dried, | |
| | freshly ground black pepper | | | or one small lettuce, washed, | |
| 1½ tbsp | virgin olive oil | 1½ tbsp | | dried and torn into pieces | |

Put the beetroot into a saucepan, pour in enough water to cover, and bring the water to the boil. Cook the beetroot until it is tender—about 30 minutes. Drain the beetroot and let it cool before peeling and finely dicing it. Put the diced beetroot in a small bowl, and toss it with 1 tablespoon of the vinegar.

To make the dressing, combine the mustards, the honey, the remaining vinegar and a liberal grinding of pepper in a bowl. Whisk in the oil.

In another bowl, toss the radicchio and chicory with two thirds of the dressing. Separately toss the lamb's lettuce with the remaining dressing.

To assemble the salad, mound the radicchio-chicory mixture in the centre of a platter and surround it with the lettuce. Scatter the diced beetroot on top.

# Chilled Celeriac, Carrot and Yellow Pepper Salad

**Serves 6 as a side dish**

**Working time: about 15 minutes**

**Total time: about 1 hour and 15 minutes**

Calories 45
Protein 1g
Cholesterol 0mg
Total fat 2g
Saturated fat 0g
Sodium 90mg

| | | | | | | |
|---|---|---|---|---|---|---|
| **250 g** | celeriac, scrubbed | **8 oz** | **1** | carrot, peeled and julienned | **1** |
| **2 tbsp** | red wine vinegar | **2 tbsp** | **1 tbsp** | safflower oil | **1 tbsp** |
| **1** | sweet yellow pepper, seeded deribbed and cut into thin strips | **1** | **¼ tsp** | sugar | **¼ tsp** |
| | | | **⅛ tsp** | salt | **⅛ tsp** |

Peel and julienne the celeriac. To prevent discoloration, transfer the pieces to a bowl and sprinkle them with the vinegar; toss the pieces well to coat them. Add the carrot, yellow pepper, oil, sugar and salt, and toss thoroughly to combine all the ingredients. Cover and refrigerate for at least 1 hour before serving.

# Chicken Salad with Barley and Mint

Serves 6 as a main course

Working time: about 45 minutes

Total time: about 3 hours and 20 minutes

Calories 410
Protein 30g
Cholesterol 80mg
Total fat 15g
Saturated fat 3g
Sodium 320mg

| | | |
|---|---|---|
| 1 kg | chicken thighs, skinned and trimmed of fat | 2 lb |
| 15 cl | fresh lemon juice | ¼ pint |
| ½ tsp | ground cumin | ½ tsp |
| ½ tsp | dry mustard | ½ tsp |
| ½ tsp | paprika | ½ tsp |
| ½ tsp | ground cinnamon | ½ tsp |
| ½ tsp | cayenne pepper | ½ tsp |
| ½ tsp | salt | ½ tsp |
| | freshly ground black pepper | |

| | | |
|---|---|---|
| 3 tbsp | chopped fresh mint, | 3 tbsp |
| 1 | garlic clove, finely chopped | 1 |
| 2 tbsp | safflower oil | 2 tbsp |
| 275 g | pearl barley | 9 oz |
| 1 litre | unsalted chicken stock | 1¾ pints |
| 1 tbsp | chopped parsley, preferably flat-leaf | 1 tbsp |
| 1 | small iceberg lettuce, washed and dried | 1 |
| | several mint sprigs | |

Put the chicken thighs in a large bowl. Combine 12.5 cl (4 fl oz) of the lemon juice, the cumin, mustard, paprika, cinnamon, cayenne pepper, salt, some black pepper, 1 tablespoon of the fresh mint, and the garlic. Pour this marinade over the thighs, and stir to coat them. Cover and marinate for 2 hours in the refrigerator.

After marinating, remove thighs from the liquid and pat them dry. Reserve the marinade. Heat the oil in a large heavy saucepan over medium heat. Add the thighs and cook until browned on all sides—about 10 minutes. Stir in the barley, the stock and 12.5 cl (4 fl oz) of marinade. Bring to the boil, then simmer until the barley is tender and most of the liquid has evaporated—about 30 minutes.

Remove the thighs; when they are cool enough to handle, chop the meat coarsley. Add the chicken to the barley, then add the parsley, the remaining mint and the remaining lemon juice. Mix the salad and serve it on a bed of iceberg lettuce, garnished with the mint sprigs.

# Crab-Potato Cakes

Serves 6
(makes 12 cakes)

Working time: about 30 minutes

Total time: about 1 hour

Calories 215
Protein 17g
Cholesterol 65mg
Total fat 8g
Saturated fat 2g
Sodium 300mg

| | | | | | | |
|---|---|---|---|---|---|---|
| 500 g | crab meat, picked over | 1 lb | $\frac{1}{4}$ tsp | salt | $\frac{1}{4}$ tsp |
| 500 g | potatoes, boiled, cooled, peeled and coarsely grated | 1 lb | $\frac{1}{4}$ tsp | freshly ground black pepper | $\frac{1}{4}$ tsp |
| | | | $\frac{1}{4}$ tsp | ground mace | $\frac{1}{4}$ tsp |
| 125 g | onion, finely chopped | 4 oz | $\frac{1}{8}$ tsp | cayenne pepper | $\frac{1}{8}$ tsp |
| 30 g | fresh parsley, finely chopped | 1 oz | 75 g | dry breadcrumbs | $2\frac{1}{2}$ oz |
| 3 tbsp | finely cut dill | 3 tbsp | 15 g | unsalted butter | $\frac{1}{2}$ oz |
| 1 tbsp | dry sherry | 1 tbsp | 2 tbsp | safflower oil | 2 tbsp |
| 2 tbsp | plain low-fat yogurt | 2 tbsp | 2 tbsp | parsley sprigs for garnish | 2 tbsp |
| 2 | egg whites, beaten | 2 | 2 | lemons, cut into wedges | 2 |

Preheat the grill. In a large mixing bowl, combine the crab meat, potatoes, onion, chopped parsley, dill, sherry, yogurt, egg whites, salt, pepper, mace and cayenne pepper; mix gently until the ingredients are thoroughly combined.

Form the mixture into 12 cakes, each about 1 cm ($\frac{1}{2}$ inch) thick. Dredge each cake in the breadcrumbs to coat it completely. Put the cakes on a lightly buttered grill pan as you

work. Melt the butter and oil together; dribble half of this mixture over the tops of the cakes.

Grill the cakes until they turn a crusty golden-brown—3 to 5 minutes. Turn the cakes over and dribble the remaining butter mixture over them. Grill the cakes for 3 to 5 minutes more. Serve immediately, garnished with the parsley sprigs and the lemon wedges.

# Haddock with Endive and Bacon

Serves 4

Working (and total) time: about 20 minutes

Calories
150
Protein
24g
Cholesterol
70mg
Total fat
3g
Saturated fat
1g
Sodium
270mg

| | | |
|---|---|---|
| **500 g** | haddock fillets (or cod or coley) | **1 lb** |
| **2** | garlic cloves, finely chopped | **2** |
| **2 tbsp** | fresh lemon juice | **2 tbsp** |
| **1 tsp** | fresh rosemary, or ¼ tsp dried rosemary, crumbled freshly ground black pepper | **1 tsp** |

| | | |
|---|---|---|
| **2** | rashers streaky bacon, rind removed | **2** |
| **1** | endive (about 500 g/1 lb), trimmed, washed and cut into 2.5 cm (1 inch) pieces | **1** |
| **⅛ tsp** | salt | **⅛ tsp** |

Rinse the haddock under cold running water and pat it dry with paper towels. Cut it into four serving pieces. Rub the fish with half of the garlic, 1 tablespoon of the lemon juice, the rosemary and a generous grinding of pepper. Set the fish aside.

Cut the rashers in half crosswise and put them in the bottom of a large dish. Microwave the bacon on high until done but not crisp—about 2 minutes. Lay a strip of bacon on top of each piece of fish.

Add the remaining garlic to the bacon fat in the dish. Add the endive to the dish with the remaining lemon juice, the salt and some pepper. Toss the endive to distribute the seasonings, then mound it in the centre of the dish. Microwave the dish on high for 2 minutes. Briefly toss the endive again and then microwave it on high until it wilts—about 2 minutes more.

Lay the fish on top of the endive. Microwave the fish on medium (50 per cent power) until the flesh is opaque—5 to 6 minutes. Remove the dish from the oven and spoon the juices that have collected in the bottom into a small saucepan. Boil the juices rapidly until only 2 tablespoons of liquid remain; pour the sauce over the fish and serve at once.

# Linguine and Chicken in Parsley Sauce

Serves 4

Working time: about 25 minutes

Total time: about 30 minutes

Calories 400
Protein 23g
Cholesterol 50mg
Total fat 13g
Saturated fat 5g
Sodium 305mg

| | | | | | | |
|---|---|---|---|---|---|---|
| 250 g | linguine (or spaghetti) | 8 oz | | $\frac{1}{4}$ litre | unsalted chicken stock | 8 fl oz |
| 1 tbsp | safflower oil | 1 tbsp | | 30 g | unsalted butter | 1 oz |
| 1 | lemon, rind only, finely julienned | 1 | | 250 g | skinned and boned chicken | 8 oz |
| 1 tsp | finely chopped fresh | 1 tsp | | | breasts, cut into cubes | |
| | ginger root | | | 2 | shallots, finely chopped | 2 |
| 1 tsp | sugar | 1 tsp | | 2 | bunches of parsley, stemmed | 2 |
| $\frac{1}{4}$ tsp | salt | $\frac{1}{4}$ tsp | | | (about 90 g/3 oz) | |

Cook the oil and lemon rind in a saucepan over medium heat for 4 minutes. Stir in the ginger, sugar and $\frac{1}{8}$ teaspoon of the salt, and cook the mixture for 3 minutes more, stirring frequently. Pour in the stock and bring the mixture to the boil; cook it until only about 12.5 cl (4 fl oz) of liquid remains—5 to 7 minutes.

Cook the linguine in 3 litres (5 pints) of boiling water with $1\frac{1}{2}$ teaspoons of salt. Start testing the pasta after 10 minutes and cook it until it is *al dente*.

While the pasta is cooking, melt 15 g ($\frac{1}{2}$ oz) of the butter in a large, heavy frying pan over medium-high heat. Add the chicken cubes and shallots; sauté them, stirring frequently, until the cubes are lightly browned—about 3 minutes. Stir in the lemon rind mixture and cook for 1 minute more. Add the parsley and cook, stirring, for an additional 3 minutes.

Drain the pasta and transfer it to a casserole. Stir the remaining butter into the sauce and combine the sauce with the pasta. Cover the casserole and let the dish stand for 5 minutes, stirring once, to meld the flavours.

# Pasta, Corn and Leek Salad

**Serves 6 as a side dish**

**Working time: about 20 minutes**

**Total time: about 30 minutes**

Calories 260
Protein 10g
Cholesterol 0mg
Total fat 4g
Saturated fat 1g
Sodium 110mg

| | | |
|---|---|---|
| **90 g** | pasta spirals | **3 oz** |
| **4** | ears of sweetcorn, husked, or | **4** |
| | 500g (1 lb) frozen sweetcorn kernels | |
| **250 g** | white parts of leek, | **8 oz** |
| | cut into thin rounds | |
| **2** | beef tomatoes, cut into thin wedges | **2** |
| **2** | black olives, stoned and diced | **2** |

| | | |
|---|---|---|
| **Mustard-basil dressing** | | |
| **1 tbsp** | fresh lemon juice | **1 tbsp** |
| **1 tsp** | Dijon mustard | **1 tsp** |
| **100 g** | low-fat fromage frais | **3½oz** |
| **¼tsp** | salt | **¼tsp** |
| | freshly ground black pepper | |
| **4 tbsp** | chopped fresh basil | **4 tbsp** |

Cook the pasta in 1 litre (1¾ pints) of boiling water with 1 teaspoon of salt. Start testing after 10 minutes and cook until it is *al dente*. Refresh the pasta under cold water, then drain.

If you are using fresh sweetcorn, cook it in a saucepan of boiling water for 6 to 10 minutes, until it is just tender. Refresh the ears under cold running water and drain them well. Using a sharp knife, cut off the corn kernels. If you are using frozen sweetcorn, blanch it in boiling water and drain it thoroughly.

Parboil the leeks for 2 to 3 minutes, until they are just tender but still have bite. Refresh them under cold running water and drain them well.

For the dressing, blend the lemon juice and mustard into the *fromage frais*, then stir in the salt, some pepper and the chopped basil. Tip the pasta, sweetcorn and leeks into a bowl, pour on the dressing and toss the salad gently to combine the ingredients. Chill the salad until required. Serve garnished with tomato wedges and olive dice.

# Cheese and Bacon Granary Bars

Serves 6

Working time: about 30 minutes

Total time: about 1 hour and 30 minutes (includes cooling)

Calories 315
Protein 12g
Cholesterol 30mg
Total fat 10g
Saturated fat 6g
Sodium 315mg

| | | |
|---|---|---|
| 45 g | rindless bacon, minced | 1½ oz |
| 150 g | granary flour | 5 oz |
| 150 g | plain flour | 5 oz |
| 3 tsp | baking powder | 3 tsp |
| ⅛ tsp | salt | ⅛ tsp |
| 45 g | unsalted butter | 1½ oz |
| 45 g | grated Cheddar cheese, | 1½ oz |
| 1 tbsp | finely grated Parmesan cheese | 1 tbsp |

| | | |
|---|---|---|
| 1 tbsp | chopped fresh oregano, | 1 tbsp |
| 1 tbsp | fresh lemon juice | 1 tbsp |
| 15 cl | skimmed milk | ¼ pint |
| | **Salad filling** | |
| 150 g | low-fat fromage frais | 5 oz |
| ¼ | crisp lettuce, sliced | ¼ |
| ¼ | cucumber, thinly sliced | ¼ |
| 6 | spring onions, sliced | 6 |

Preheat the oven to 230°C (450°F or Mark 8), and grease and flour a baking sheet.

Dry-fry the bacon until lightly browned. Cool on paper towels.

Sift the granary flour with the plain flour, baking powder and salt. Rub in the butter until the mixture resembles fine breadcrumbs. Stir in the bacon, Cheddar and Parmesan and the oregano. Add the lemon juice to the milk then less gradually mix sufficient liquid into the dry ingredients to make a soft, but not sticky, dough.

Transfer the dough to a floured work surface and shape it into a rectangle measuring about 25 by 10 cm (10 by 4 inches). Lift the dough on to the prepared baking sheet. Mark the top of the dough into six bars, cutting into the dough. Bake until well risen, firm to the touch and golden—about 20 minutes. Cool on a wire rack.

Cut the bread into the six marked bars and split each one in half. Fill the bars with the *fromage frais* and the lettuce, cucumber and spring onion slices.

# Wholemeal Loaf Filled with Smoked Chicken Salad

Serves 8

Working time:
about 1 hour

Total time:
about 9 hours
(includes
chilling)

Calories
190
Protein
22g
Cholesterol
45mg
Total fat
5g
Saturated fat
2g
Sodium
400mg

| | | |
|---|---|---|
| **500 g** | boned and skinned cooked | **1 lb** |
| | smoked chicken breasts, cut | |
| | crosswise into thin slices, or one 1.5 kg | |
| | (3 lb) cooked smoked chicken, skinned | |
| | and boned, meat cut into thin slices | |
| **4** | garlic cloves, crushed | **4** |
| **1** | round wholemeal loaf, 18 cm | **1** |
| | (7 inches) in diameter | |

| | | |
|---|---|---|
| **15 g** | unsalted butter | **½ oz** |
| **125 g** | sorrel leaves, washed, dried | **4 oz** |
| | and trimmed | |
| **4** | firm small tomatoes | **4** |
| | (about 275 g/9 oz), thinly sliced | |
| **¼** | cucumber; thinly sliced | **¼** |
| **½ tsp** | salt | **½ tsp** |
| | freshly ground black pepper | |

Cut a lid, about 12 cm (5 inches) in diameter, from the top of the loaf. Scoop out most of the crumb from the centre, leaving a crusty shell about 1 cm (½ inch) thick. Using the back of a dessertspoon, spread the butter inside the shell and on the underside of the lid.

Lay about one quarter of the sorrel leaves in the base of the hollowed-out loaf, and spread them with one quarter of the crushed garlic. Pack one third of the sliced chicken on top, followed by one third of the tomato and cucumber slices. Season with a little of the

salt and plenty of freshly ground black pepper. Repeat the layers with the remaining ingredients, finishing with a layer of sorrel and garlic.

Place the buttered lid over the top layer of filling, and wrap the loaf in foil. Set a bread board on top of the loaf, and weight it down with a 1 kg (2 lb) weight from a kitchen scale. Chill the loaf overnight.

To serve, remove the foil and cut the loaf into wedges, using a sharp knife.

# Melon and Parma Ham in Poppy Seed Rolls

Makes 6 filled rolls

Working (and total) time: about 20 minutes

Per filled roll:
Calories
218
Protein
7g
Cholesterol
50mg
Total fat
9g
Saturated fat
4g
Sodium
470mg

| | | | | | | |
|---|---|---|---|---|---|---|
| 6 | crusty poppy-seed rolls | 6 | | 12 | thin cucumber slices, halved | 12 |
| 6 tbsp | cream cheese | 6 tbsp | | 6 | paper-thin slices Parma ham | 6 |
| 45 g | piece of peeled melon, cut into six slices | 1½ oz | | 12 | (about 45 g/1½ oz) watercress sprigs | 12 |

Cut the rolls in half and spread 1 tablespoon of the cream cheese evenly over each bottom half. Arrange a melon slice and four pieces of cucumber on the cheese in each roll, and lay a slice of Parma ham on top of the melon. Add two sprigs of watercress to each roll and replace the top halves.

# Spicy Cod and Corn in Sourdough Bread

Makes 6
sandwiches

Working time:
about 30
minutes

Total time:
about 1 hour
and 30
minutes

Per sandwich:
Calories
200
Protein
11g
Cholesterol
15mg
Total fat
7g
Saturated fat
1g
Sodium
350mg

| | | | |
|---|---|---|---|
| 140 g | cod fillet | 4½ oz | |
| 30 cl | unsalted vegetable stock | ½ pint | |
| 1 tbsp | mayonnaise | 1 tbsp | |
| 2 tbsp | thick Greek yogurt | 2 tbsp | |
| ½ tsp | garam masala | ½ tsp | |
| ½ tsp | ground turmeric | ½ tsp | |
| 12 | slices sourdough bread | 12 | |
| 90 g | frozen sweetcorn kernels, blanched in boiling water and drained thoroughly | 3 oz | |
| 6 | unskinned shelled almonds, cut into slivers with a sharp knife | 6 | |
| ½ | box mustard and cress, trimmed | ½ | |

Place the fish in a wide, shallow pan, and pour in sufficient stock to cover it. Cover the pan, and bring the liquid gently to simmering point.

Simmer the cod for 3 to 4 minutes, until the flesh flakes easily with a fork. Using a fish slice, transfer the cod to a plate and allow it to cool. Flake the fish gently.

Place the mayonnaise and yogurt in a small bowl, and stir in the garam masala and turmeric. Spread this mixture evenly over six of the bread slices. Divide the flaked cod and the sweetcorn among the six covered slices, and sprinkle on a few almond slivers. Top each filling with some mustard and cress and cover it with a second slice of bread.

# Chicken, Celery and Pistachio Nut Baps

Makes 6 filled baps

Working (and total) time: about 25 minutes

Per filled bap:
Calories 200
Protein 15g
Cholesterol 20mg
Total fat 4g
Saturated fat 1g
Sodium 360mg

| | | |
|---|---|---|
| **6** | wholemeal baps | **6** |
| **175 g** | skinned cooked chicken breast, cut into strips | **6 oz** |
| **1 tbsp** | whole grain mustard | **1 tbsp** |
| **6** | iceberg lettuce leaves, washed and dried | **6** |

| | | |
|---|---|---|
| **6 tbsp** | low-fat fromage frais | **6 tbsp** |
| **2** | small sticks celery, trimmed and thinly sliced | **2** |
| **18** | skinned shelled pistachio nuts, finely sliced cayenne pepper, for garnish | **18** |

Cut the baps in half and spread each bottom half evenly with 1 tablespoon of the *fromage frais*. Spread the mustard over the chicken breast strips.

Place a lettuce leaf on top of each covered base and divide the chicken strips, celery slices and pistachio nuts among them. Garnish each filling with a light dusting of cayenne pepper and replace the top halves of the baps.

# Chocolate Kisses

Makes 36
kisses

Working time:
about 40
minutes

Total time:
about 50
minutes

Per kiss:
Calories
65
Protein
1g
Cholesterol
0mg
Total fat
2g
Saturated fat
1g
Sodium
5mg

| | | |
|---|---|---|
| **60 g** | plain chocolate, broken into pieces | **2 oz** |
| **125 g** | blanched almonds, toasted and finely ground | **4 oz** |
| **125 g** | shelled hazelnuts, toasted and skinned, finely ground | **4 oz** |
| **90 g** | cornmeal | **3 oz** |

| | | |
|---|---|---|
| **90 g** | icing sugar | **3 oz** |
| **90 g** | caster sugar | **3 oz** |
| **1 tbsp** | clear honey | **1 tbsp** |
| **2** | egg whites | **2** |
| **5 tbsp** | apricot jam without added sugar | **5 tbsp** |

Preheat the oven to 220°C (425°F or Mark 7). Line two large baking sheets with non-stick parchment paper.

Melt the chocolate in a heatproof bowl set over a pan of simmering water. Place the nuts, cornmeal, icing sugar, caster sugar and honey in a mixing bowl. Add the melted chocolate and stir thoroughly, then add the egg whites and mix to a stiff batter.

Spoon the mixture into a piping bag fitted with a 5 mm (¼ inch) star nozzle. Pipe 72 rosettes, each about 4 cm (1½ inches) in diameter, at least 2.5 cm (1 inch) apart, on to the prepared baking sheets.

Bake the rosettes until set—8 to 10 minutes—then transfer to wire racks and cool. Just before serving, sandwich the rosettes together in pairs with the jam.

# Chicken Breasts Stuffed with Garlic and Carrots

| | | |
|---|---|---|
| Serves 4 | | |
| Working time: about 45 minutes | | |
| Total time: about 1 hour | | |

| | | |
|---|---|---|
| Calories 245 | | |
| Protein 28g | | |
| Cholesterol 75mg | | |
| Total fat 9g | | |
| Saturated fat 2g | | |
| Sodium 360mg | | |

| | | | | | |
|---|---|---|---|---|---|
| 4 | chicken breasts, skinned and boned (about 500 g/1 lb) | 4 | ½ tsp | salt | ½ tsp |
| 1 tbsp | virgin olive oil | 1 tbsp | 2 tbsp | fresh rosemary leaves | 2 tbsp |
| 24 to 32 | garlic cloves, peeled | 24 to 32 | 1 tsp | safflower oil | 1 tsp |
| 1 | large carrot, cut into 12 strips 5 mm (¼ inch) thick and 10 cm (4 inches) long | 1 | | freshly ground black pepper | |
| | | | 12.5 cl | unsalted chicken stock | 4 fl oz |
| | | | 4 tbsp | dry white wine | 4 tbsp |
| | | | 1 | shallot finely chopped | 1 |

Cook the garlic cloves gently in the olive oil, stirring occasionally, for 20 minutes. Sprinkle with ⅛ teaspoon of the salt and cook until golden-brown—10 minutes more. Remove with a slotted spoon. Keep the oil in the frying pan.

Blanch the carrot strips in boiling water for 4 minutes then drain and set aside. Lay the chicken breasts on a cutting board, smooth sides down. Along the thinner long edge of each breast, slice horizontally nearly through to the opposite side. Open out each breast into two flaps. Sprinkle on the rosemary and ¼ teaspoon of the salt. Arrange three carrot

strips on each larger flap, and distribute the garlic cloves in between. Press the breasts as nearly closed as possible.

Heat the safflower oil with the oil in the pan over medium high. Sauté the breasts on one side until browned—about 5 minutes. Turn gently and sprinkle with the remaining seasoning. Cook on the second side until firm but springy to the touch—5 to 7 minutes more. Remove the breasts and place on a warmed platter.

Stir stock, wine and shallot into the pan juices to deglaze it. Stir until reduced by half. Pour some sauce over each breast and serve.

# Penne with Provençal Vegetables

Serves 4

Working (and total) time: about 40 minutes

Calories 335
Protein 11g
Cholesterol 5mg
Total fat 7g
Saturated fat 1g
Sodium 185mg

| | | | | | |
|---|---|---|---|---|---|
| 250 g | penne | 8 oz | ¼ tsp | finely chopped fresh rosemary | ¼ tsp |
| 250 g | aubergine | 8 oz | ¼ tsp | fresh thyme | ¼ tsp |
| 2 | courgettes | 2 | ⅛ tsp | fennel seeds | ⅛ tsp |
| 2 | sweet red peppers, cut into 1 cm (½ inch) squares | 2 | ¼ tsp | salt | ¼ tsp |
| 3 | garlic cloves, thinly sliced | 3 | | freshly ground black pepper | |
| 2 tbsp | chopped fresh parsley | 2 tbsp | 2 tbsp | virgin olive oil | 2 tbsp |
| ¼ tsp | fresh oregano | ¼ tsp | ½ litre | unsalted chicken stock | 16 fl oz |
| | | | ¼ litre | unsalted tomato juice | 8 fl oz |

Halve the aubergine and the courgettes lengthwise, then cut them lengthwise again into wedges about 1 cm (½ inch) wide. Slice the wedges into 2.5 cm (1 inch) long pieces. Place in a baking dish along with the red pepper, garlic, parsley, oregano, rosemary, thyme, fennel seeds, salt and some pepper. Cover and microwave on high for 2 minutes. Rotate the dish half a turn and microwave it on high until the vegetables are barely tender—about 2 minutes more. Stir in the oil.

In a deep bowl, combine the penne, stock and tomato juice. If necessary, add just enough water to immerse the pasta in liquid. Cover the bowl, and microwave on high, stirring the pasta every 2 minutes, until it is *al dente*—about 15 minutes. With a slotted spoon, transfer the pasta to the baking dish with the vegetable mixture and stir to combine. Pour about half of the pasta cooking liquid into the dish, then cover the dish and microwave it on high for 2 minutes more to heat it through. Serve at once.

51

# Cannelloni with Cottage Cheese and Courgettes

**Serves 6**

Working time:
about 35
minutes

Total time:
about 1 hour
and 30
minutes

Calories
380
Protein
24g
Cholesterol
30mg
Total fat
11g
Saturated fat
7g
Sodium
590mg

| | | |
|---|---|---|
| 12 | cannelloni tubes | 12 |
| 30 g | unsalted butter | 1 oz |
| 3 | large shallots, finely chopped | 3 |
| 2 | garlic cloves, finely chopped | 2 |
| 1 | medium carrot, grated | 1 |
| 1 | medium courgette, sliced | 1 |
| 800 g | canned tomatoes, chopped the juice reserved | 28 oz |
| 4 tbsp | tomato paste | 4 tbsp |
| 1 tbsp | chopped fresh oregano, | 1 tbsp |

| | | |
|---|---|---|
| 2 tbsp | chopped fresh basil leaves | 2 tbsp |
| 2 tbsp | dark brown sugar | 2 tbsp |
| | freshly ground black pepper | |
| $\frac{1}{4}$ tsp | salt | $\frac{1}{4}$ tsp |
| 350 g | low-fat cottage cheese | 12 oz |
| 125 g | mozzarella, grated | 4 oz |
| 3 | egg whites | 3 |
| 3 tbsp | chopped fresh parsley | 3 tbsp |
| 60 g | Parmesan cheese, freshly grated | 2 oz |
| | fresh basil sprigs for garnish | |

Melt the butter in a large bowl in the microwave. Add the shallots, garlic, carrot and courgette; toss, then microwave on medium high for 4 minutes. Add the tomatoes and their juice, tomato paste, oregano, basil, brown sugar, seasoning, and stir well. Cover the bowl loosely and microwave on medium high for 12 minutes, stirring every 4 minutes.

Stir together the cheeses, egg whites and parsley. Fill the tubes with the mixture.

Reheat the sauce, then spread half over the bottom of a shallow dish. Lay the cannelloni in the sauce and the remaining sauce. Cover and microwave on high for 10 minutes, then turn each tube over. Microwave on medium high for 17 minutes more. Leave to stand for 12 minutes. Garnish with basil.

# Baked Plums with Streusel Topping

Serves 8

Working time: about 30 minutes

Total time: about 45 minutes

Calories 185
Protein 2g
Cholesterol 8mg
Total fat 6g
Saturated fat 2g
Sodium 5mg

| 8 | ripe purple plums, quartered and stoned | 8 |
|---|---|---|
| ½ litre | brandy | 8 fl oz |
| 4 tbsp | dark brown sugar | 4 tbsp |
| 1 | orange, grated rind only | 1 |

| | Streusel topping | |
|---|---|---|
| 4 tbsp | oatmeal | 4 tbsp |
| 4 tbsp | plain flour | 4 tbsp |
| 30 g | unsalted butter, softened | 1 oz |
| 5 tbsp | dark brown sugar | 5 tbsp |
| 4 tbsp | finely chopped walnuts | 4 tbsp |
| 1 | orange, grated rind only | 1 |

Arrange the plum quarters skin side up in a 20 cm (8 inch) square baking dish. Preheat the oven to 200°C (400°F or Mark 6).

Combine the brandy, brown sugar and orange rind a small saucepan. Bring the mixture to the boil, then cook it until the liquid is reduced to 4 tablespoons—about 5 minutes. Pour the brandy syrup evenly over the plums.

To make the streusel topping, chop the oatmeal in a food processor or a blender until it is as fine as flour. Transfer the chopped oatmeal to a large bowl and mix in the flour, butter, brown sugar, walnuts and rind. Dot the surface of the plums with spoonfuls of the topping. Bake the plums until the streusel has browned and the fruit juices are bubbling— 15 to 20 minutes.

# Baked Apples Filled with Cranberries and Sultanas

**Serves 6**

**Working time: about 20 minutes**

**Total time: about 40 minutes**

Calories
210
Protein
1g
Cholesterol
8mg
Total fat
4g
Saturated fat
2g
Sodium
8mg

| | | | | | | |
|---|---|---|---|---|---|---|
| **250 g** | fresh or frozen cranberries | **8 oz** | **25 g** | unsalted butter | **¾ oz** |
| **90 g** | light brown sugar | **3 oz** | **6** | Golden Delicious | **6** |
| **3 tbsp** | sultanas, chopped | **3 tbsp** | | apples | |

Put the cranberries into a glass bowl and sprinkle the brown sugar over them. Cover the bowl with plastic film and microwave the berries on high for 2 minutes. Stir in the sultanas and 15 g (½ oz) of the butter, recover the bowl, and cook the mixture on high until the berries start to burst—1½ to 2 ½ minutes. Stir the mixture well and set it aside.

Core one of the apples with a melon baller or a small spoon, scooping out the centre of the apple to form a conical cavity 3 cm (1¼ inches) wide at the top and only 1 cm (½ inch) wide at the bottom. Using a cannelle knife or a paring knife, cut two grooves for decoration

round the apple. Prepare the other apples the same way.

Fill the apples with the cranberry mixture. Arrange the apples in a ring round the edge of a glass pie plate and dot them with the remaining butter. Cover the filled apples with greaseproof paper and microwave them on high for 5 minutes. Rotate the plate and each apple 180 degrees, and microwave the apples on high for 3 to 5 minutes more. Let the apples stand for about 5 minutes before serving them with their baking juices ladled over the top.

# Harlequins

Makes 24
harlequins

Working time:
about 1 hour
and 10 minutes

Total time
about 2 hours
(includes
chilling)

Calories
60
Protein
1g
Cholesterol
20mg
Total fat
2g
Saturated fat
1g
Sodium
10mg

| | | |
|---|---|---|
| 3 | peaches, halved and stoned | 3 |
| 250 g | fresh raspberries | 8 oz |
| 250 g | fresh blackcurrants, topped and tailed | 8 oz |
| 3 tbsp | caster sugar | 3 tbsp |
| 2 tbsp | powdered gelatine | 2 tbsp |
| 6 tbsp | fromage frais | 6 tbsp |
| | peach slices, raspberries and blackcurrants, to decorate | |

| Genoese sponge | | |
|---|---|---|
| 2 | eggs | 2 |
| 1 | egg white | 1 |
| 90 g | caster sugar | 3 oz |
| 90 g | plain flour | 3 oz |
| 15 g | unsalted butter, melted and cooled | ½ oz |

Prepare a genoese sponge with the ingredients listed above; bake for 10 to 15 minutes only, then unmould and cool.

Put the peaches, raspberries and blackcurrants into three separate saucepans, each with 2 tablespoons of water and 1 tablespoon of the caster sugar. Cook them gently, until the fruits are tender—3 to 4 minutes. Purée then sieve separately.

Dissolve the gelatine in 6 tablespoons of water in a bowl set over a pan of simmering water. Stir one third of the solution into each purée, then whisk 2 tablespoons *fromage frais* into each.

Refrigerate until nearly set—10 to 15 minutes.

Meanwhile, line the baking tin in which the sponge was cooked with a piece of foil overlapping the rim on the two short sides. Replace the sponge.

Spread the blackcurrant mixture over the sponge, then chill it for 5 minutes. Spread on a peach layer and chill again, repeat with the raspberry mixture. Chill until set.

Lift the sponge out of the tin using the foil handles. Peel back the foil and trim the assembly, then cut into shapes. Decorate with fruit.

# Lasagnette with Chicken, Mango and Raisins

Serves 4

Working time:
about 20
minutes

Total time
about 1 hour

Calories
465
Protein
32g
Cholesterol
90mg
Total fat
8g
Saturated fat
2g
Sodium
200mg

| | | | | | |
|---|---|---|---|---|---|
| 250 g | narrow lasagnette | 8 oz | 1 | large onion, chopped finely | 1 |
| 6 | chicken drumsticks, skinned and boned, the meat cut into 2.5 cm (1 inch) pieces | 6 | 4 | garlic cloves, crushed | 4 |
| | | | ¼ tsp | salt | ¼ tsp |
| | | | 35 cl | unsalted chicken stock | 12 fl oz |
| ⅛ tsp | cayenne pepper | ⅛ tsp | 1 | mango, peeled, the flesh cut into neat cubes | 1 |
| ¼ tsp | each ground cloves, cinnamon, cardamom and cumin | ¼ tsp | | | |
| 1 tsp | ground turmeric | 1 tsp | 30 g | raisins | 1 oz |
| 1 tbsp | virgin olive oil | 1 tbsp | 2 tbsp | finely chopped parsley | 2 tbsp |

Put the chicken pieces into a mixing bowl, sprinkle with the spices and toss well to coat evenly. Cover the bowl and let it stand at room temperature for at least 30 minutes.

Heat the oil in a large, heavy-bottomed sauté pan over medium heat, tilting the pan to coat it evenly Add the onion and garlic and sauté them, stirring constantly, until the onion is translucent—about 3 minutes. Sprinkle the salt over the chicken, then add the pieces to the pan. Sauté, stirring frequently, for about 5 minutes, until the chicken is very lightly browned. Pour the stock into the pan and bring to the boil. Add the mango and raisins. Reduce the heat, partially cover the pan and simmer gently for 20 minutes.

Meanwhile, cook the lasagnette in 3 litres (5 pints) of boiling water with 1½ teaspoons of salt. Start testing after 10 minutes and cook until they are *al dente*.

Drain the pasta well, then put it into a large heated serving bowl. Add the chicken mixture and the parsley. Toss gently together and serve immediately.

# Pork Hotpot

Serves 8

Working time:
about 40
minutes

Total time:
about 4 hours
and 30 minutes
(includes
soaking)

Calories
365
Protein
25g
Cholesterol
70mg
Total fat
9g
Saturated fat
3g
Sodium
400mg

| | | | | | | |
|---|---|---|---|---|---|---|
| **1 kg** | pork fillet, trimmed of fat and cut into chunks | **2 lb** | | **1.5 kg** | new potatoes, scrubbed and sliced | **3 lb** |
| **¾ litre** | dry cider | **1¼ pints** | | **250 g** | small carrots, halved crosswise and then quartered lengthwise | **8 oz** |
| **2** | cinnamon sticks | **2** | | | | |
| **12** | allspice berries | **12** | | **500 g** | small leeks, sliced | **1 lb** |
| **16** | cloves | **16** | | **2** | sticks celery, chopped | **2** |
| **24** | black peppercorns | **24** | | **60 g** | sultanas | **2 oz** |
| **2** | oranges, pared rind only | **2** | | **1 tsp** | salt | **1 tsp** |
| **125 g** | dried pears | **4 oz** | | | | |

Put the cider in a non-reactive saucepan with the cinnamon, allspice, cloves, peppercorns and orange rind and bring to the boil. Remove the pan from the heat, cover and leave to infuse for 30 minutes.

Add the pears to the spiced cider and set aside to soak, uncovered, for 1 hour.

Lift out the pears and cut them into strips crosswise, then set them aside. Strain and reserve the soaking liquid, and discard the spices and flavourings.

Preheat the oven to 170°C (325°F or Mark 3). Grease the bottom of a casserole. Lay one third of the potato over the bottom, then layer the carrots, pork, leeks, celery and sultanas in the casserole. Scatter the strips of pear over the top. Stir the salt into the reserved spiced cider and pour it into the casserole, then arrange the remaining potato slices on top.

Cover the casserole and cook the hotpot in the oven for 1¾ hours. Take it out of the oven and remove the lid. Tilt the casserole and spoon some liquid over the top layer of potatoes. Return the casserole to the oven, uncovered, and cook for a further 40 minutes to brown the surface.

# Turkey Escalopes with Red and Green Peppers

**Serves 4**

**Working time:**
about 15
minutes

**Total time:**
about 30
minutes

Calories
235
Protein
27g
Cholesterol
60mg
Total fat
11g
Saturated fat
2g
Sodium
205mg

| | | |
|---|---|---|
| 8 | 5 mm (¼ inch) thick turkey escalopes (about 500 g/1 lb), pounded to 3 mm (⅛ inch) thickness | 8 |
| 60 g | plain flour | 2 oz |
| 2 tbsp | safflower oil | 2 tbsp |
| 1 tsp | virgin olive oil | 1 tsp |
| 4 tbsp | finely chopped onion | 4 tbsp |
| 2 | garlic cloves, finely chopped | 2 |

| | | |
|---|---|---|
| 17.5 cl | unsalted turkey stock | 6 fl oz |
| 2 tbsp | chopped fresh basil or | 2 tbsp |
| 2 tbsp | balsamic vinegar, or 1 tbsp red wine vinegar | 2 tbsp |
| ¼ tsp | salt | ¼ tsp |
| | freshly ground black pepper | |
| 1 | large sweet green pepper, julienned | 1 |
| 1 | large sweet red pepper, julienned | 1 |

To prevent the turkey from curling, score the edges of the escalopes with 3 mm (⅛ inch) slits at 2.5 to 5 cm (1 to 2 inch) intervals. Dredge the escalopes in the flour and shake off the excess.

Heat a large, heavy frying pan over medium-high heat and add half of the safflower oil. Put four escalopes in the pan and sauté them for 45 seconds. Turn them over and sauté them until their edges turn from pink to white—about 30 seconds more. Transfer the cooked escalopes to a heated platter. Add the remaining tablespoon of safflower oil to the pan and sauté the other

four escalopes. Remove the pan from the heat and transfer the turkey to the platter. Cover loosely with aluminium foil and keep warm.

To prepare the peppers, reduce the heat to medium low and heat the olive oil in the pan. Add the onion and garlic and cook until the onion is translucent—about 10 minutes. Then add the stock, basil, vinegar, salt, pepper and julienned peppers. Increase the heat to medium and simmer until the peppers are tender—about 5 minutes. Spoon the pepper mixture over the escalopes and serve the dish immediately.

# Turkey Escalopes with Pine-Nuts and Currants

Serves 4

Working (and total) time: about 50 minutes

Calories
450
Protein
33g
Cholesterol
60mg
Total fat
26g
Saturated fat
4g
Sodium
485mg

| | | |
|---|---|---|
| **8** | 5 mm ($\frac{1}{4}$ inch) thick turkey breast escalopes (about 500g/1 lb), pounded to 3 mm ($\frac{1}{8}$ inch) thickness | **8** |
| **3** | egg whites | **3** |
| **$\frac{1}{2}$ tsp** | salt | **$\frac{1}{2}$ tsp** |
| | freshly ground black pepper | |
| **3 tbsp** | virgin olive oil | **3 tbsp** |
| **3 tbsp** | finely chopped shallots | **3 tbsp** |
| **8 cl** | white wine vinegar | **3 fl oz** |
| **10** | black peppercorns | **10** |

| | | |
|---|---|---|
| **3** | bay leaves | **3** |
| **3 tbsp** | currants | **3 tbsp** |
| **8 cl** | safflower oil | **3 fl oz** |
| **60 g** | dry breadcrumbs | **2 fl oz** |
| **30 g** | fresh parsley, finely chopped | **1 oz** |
| **2** | garlic cloves, finely chopped | **2** |
| **$\frac{1}{2}$** | orange, rind only, finely chopped or grated | **$\frac{1}{2}$** |
| **3 tbsp** | pine-nuts, lightly toasted | **3 tbsp** |

In a shallow bowl, beat the egg whites with the salt and pepper. Add the escalopes one at a time, turning them to coat them with the mixture.

In a small heavy-bottomed saucepan, heat the olive oil. Add the shallots and sauté over medium heat until translucent—about 5 minutes. Add the vinegar, 17.5 cl (6 fl oz) water, peppercorns and bay leaves, and simmer for 20 minutes. Stir in the currants and simmer for another 10 minutes, or until the liquid is reduced by half, to about 12.5 cl (4 fl oz).

In the meantime, heat the safflower oil in a large heavy frying pan. Spread the breadcrumbs on a plate. Dip the escalopes in the crumbs, then brown them in the hot oil over medium to high heat for 1 to 2 minutes on each side. Put them on a heated platter and cover with foil to keep warm.

To assemble, combine the parsley, garlic and rind. Strain the reduced sauce, reserving the currants, and pour it evenly over the turkey escalopes. Sprinkle with the currants, the parsley mixture and the pine-nuts. Serve warm or, if preferred, at room temperature.

# Broccoli-Studded Prawns

Serves 4

Working (and total) time: about 30 minutes

Calories
160
Protein
17g
Cholesterol
130mg
Total fat
8g
Saturated fat
1g
Sodium
155mg

| | | | | | | |
|---|---|---|---|---|---|---|
| 24 | Mediterranean prawns (about 600 g/1¼ lb), peeled, tails left on | 24 | 2 tsp | finely chopped fresh ginger root | 2 tsp |
| 24 | broccoli florets each stem trimmed to 2.5 cm (1 inch) long and tapered to a point, blanched for 1 minute | 24 | 2 tbsp | rice vinegar | 2 tbsp |
| | | | 2 tbsp | rice wine or dry sherry | 2 tbsp |
| 2 | spring onions, trimmed and chopped | 2 | 1 tsp | chili paste with garlic | 1 tsp |
| | | | 1 tsp | tomato paste | 1 tsp |
| 1 | garlic clove, finely chopped | 1 | 1 tsp | cornflour, mixed with 2 tbsp water | 1 tsp |
| | | | 2 tbsp | safflower oil | 2 tbsp |

Using a skewer, make a 5 mm (¼ inch) diameter hole through each prawn from front to back, about one third of the way from its larger end. Insert a broccoli stem into the hole so that the floret nestles within the curve of the prawn, as shown. Transfer the prawns to a bowl with the spring onions, garlic and ginger; toss the mixture gently and let it stand for 10 minutes.

While the prawns are marinating, combine the vinegar, rice wine or sherry, chili paste,

tomato paste and the cornflour mixture in a small bowl. Set aside.

Heat the oil in a wok or heavy frying pan over medium-high heat. Add half the prawns and gently stir-fry them until they are opaque and firm—about 2 minutes. Remove and keep warm. Stir-fry the second batch. Return the first batch to the wok and pour in the sauce. Stirring gently to coat the prawns, cook until the sauce thickens—about 1 minute.

# Lamb and Broccoli Stir-Fry

Serves 4

Working (and total) time: about 25 minutes

Calories 245
Protein 22g
Cholesterol 50mg
Total fat 8g
Saturated fat 3g
Sodium 270mg

| | | |
|---|---|---|
| 350 g | lean lamb (from the loin), cut into thin strips | 12 oz |
| 4 tsp | safflower oil | 4 tsp |
| 20 g | fermented black beans, soaked in water for 5 minutes | ¾ oz |
| ½ tsp | sesame oil | ½ tsp |
| 1 | onion, halved lengthwise, cut into strips | 1 |
| 2 | garlic cloves, finely chopped | 2 |
| 2.5 cm | piece fresh ginger root, finely chopped | 1 inch |

| | | |
|---|---|---|
| 175 g | broccoli, blanched, stalks peeled and julienned, flowers divided into florets | 6 oz |
| 2 | sticks celery, chopped | 2 |
| 1 | sweet red pepper, seeded, deribbed and thinly sliced | 1 |
| 1 tsp | low-sodium soy sauce or shoyu | 1 tsp |
| 200 g | fresh water chestnuts, peeled and boiled for 3 minutes, or canned water chestnuts, drained | 7 oz |
| 3 tbsp | medium sherry | 3 tbsp |

Heat 1 teaspoon of the safflower oil in a wok or a large heavy frying pan and stir-fry half of the lamb over a medium heat, tossing and stirring until it is browned—about 2 minutes. Remove the lamb from the wok and keep it warm. Heat another teaspoon of the oil in the wok, stir-fry the remaining meat and add it to the first batch.

Drain the black beans and mash them in a small bowl with the sesame oil to make a coarse paste. Set aside. Put the remaining safflower oil into the wok or frying pan, add the onion, chopped garlic and ginger and stir-fry for 1 minute. Add the broccoli, celery, red pepper and soy sauce and stir-fry for a further 2 minutes. Add the water chestnuts, black bean paste and sherry, and return the lamb to the wok. Stir-fry over medium heat for a further 2 minutes, so that all the ingredients are coated with the sauce and heated through. Serve immediately.

# Roast Shoulder with Rosemary

**Serves 12**

**Working time: about 40 minutes**

**Total time: about 3 hours (includes marinating)**

**Calories 310**

**Protein 20g**

**Cholesterol 75mg**

**Total fat 12g**

**Saturated fat 5g**

**Sodium 130mg**

| | | |
|---|---|---|
| **2.5 kg** | shoulder of lamb, trimmed of fat | **3 lb** |
| **1 tbsp** | virgin olive oil | **1 tbsp** |
| **2 tsp** | mixed dried herbs | **2 tsp** |
| **½ tsp** | salt | **½ tsp** |
| **4** | long rosemary sprigs | **4** |
| **1½ tsp** | plain flour | **1½ tsp** |
| **60 cl** | unsalted chicken or brown stock | **1 pint** |
| | freshly ground black pepper | |

Make four diagonal incisions with a sharp knife across the shoulder, almost down to the bone. Rub the olive oil, mixed herbs and salt all over the lamb, then insert the rosemary sprigs in the diagonal cuts. Place the shoulder in a roasting pan and set it aside in a cool place to marinate for 1 hour. Preheat the oven to 220°C (425°F or Mark 7).

Roast the shoulder for 15 minutes, then reduce the oven temperature to 190°C (375°F or Mark 5) and roast the meat for a further 45 minutes to 1 hour for rare to medium meat, basting frequently with the pan juices. Transfer the shoulder to a serving dish, cover it loosely with foil and set it aside to rest in a warm place while you make the gravy.

Tip the roasting pan slightly so that the juices run to one corner, then skim off any fat. Sprinkle the flour over the juices left in the pan and stir well with a wooden spoon until the juices and flour are smoothly blended. Gradually add the stock, stirring continuously. Place the pan over moderate heat and bring the gravy to the boil, stirring all the time until it thickens; season with some black pepper. Reduce the heat to low and simmer for 6 to 8 minutes, stirring occasionally. Strain the gravy through a sieve into a warmed gravy boat and serve it with the roast shoulder.

# Lamb and Apple Casserole

| | | |
|---|---|---|
| Serves 4 | | Calories 430 |
| Working time: about 30 minutes | | Protein 40g |
| | | Cholesterol 75mg |
| Total time: about 2 hours and 25 minutes | | Total fat 10g |
| | | Saturated fat 5g |
| | | Sodium 290mg |

| | | | | | | |
|---|---|---|---|---|---|---|
| **500 g** | lean lamb (from the loin), trimmed of fat and cut into thin slices | **1 lb** | **½ tsp** | salt freshly ground black pepper | **½ tsp** |
| **750 g** | potatoes, very thinly sliced | **1½ lb** | **600 g** | dessert apples, peeled, cored and sliced | **1¼ lb** |
| **2 tsp** | finely chopped fresh sage, or ½ tsp dried sage | **2 tsp** | **1** | large onion, sliced into very thin rings | **1** |
| **1** | orange, finely grated rind and juice | **1** | **15 cl** | dry cider | **¼ pint** |

Preheat the oven to 180°C (350°F or Mark 4). Arrange half of the potato slices in the bottom of a 2.5 litre (4 pint) casserole. Sprinkle them with a little of the sage, orange rind and salt, and plenty of black pepper.

Cover the potatoes with half the apple slices; season this layer in the same way.

Continue to build up the casserole in layers as follows, seasoning each layer with some of the sage, orange rind, salt and pepper. Arrange the slices of lamb evenly over the apple, and spread the onion rings over the lamb, leaving a small space uncovered in the centre of the layer. Cover the onion with the remaining apples, and top the casserole with the remaining potatoes, maintaining the small gap in the centre of both layers and overlapping the slices of potato on the top layer in neat concentric circles.

Mix the orange juice and cider together and pour the liquid slowly into the hole in the centre of the potato topping. Cover and cook the casserole in the oven for 1½ hours, then remove the lid and continue cooking until the ingredients feel tender when pierced with a fine skewer and the potato topping is golden-brown—30 to 45 minutes. Serve the casserole hot, straight from the dish.

# Baguette and Brie Bake

Serves 4

Working time:
about 10
minutes

Total time:
about 40
minutes

Calories
220
Protein
14g
Cholesterol
80mg
Total fat
8g
Saturated fat
1g
Sodium
460mg

| | | | | | |
|---|---|---|---|---|---|
| **100 g** | Brie or Camembert cheese, chilled | **3½ oz** | **2** | egg whites | **2** |
| **1** | small baguette (about 175 g/6 oz) | **1** | **20 cl** | semi-skimmed milk | **7 fl oz** |
| **1** | egg | **1** | | freshly ground black pepper | |

Preheat the oven to 180°C (350°F or Mark 4). Lightly grease a large, shallow ovenproof dish.

Using a sharp knife, slice the cheese lengthwise into 5 mm (¼ inch) thick slices, then cut each slice into pieces about 3 cm (1¼ inch) wide, to give 16 small slices. Cut the baguette into 16 slices.

Fit the slices of bread and cheese alternately into the prepared dish. Beat the egg and egg whites in a bowl, add the milk and some black pepper, then carefully pour the mixture over the bread and cheese, ensuring that all the bread is thoroughly soaked.

Place the dish in the oven and bake for 30 minutes, until the surface is golden-brown and crisp, and the custard is just firm in the centre. Serve at once with a mixed green salad.

# Oven-Baked French Fries

Serves 4

Working time:
about 15
minutes

Total time:
about 1 hour

Calories
105
Protein
2g
Cholesterol
0mg
Total fat
3g
Saturated fat
0g
Sodium
145mg

| | | | | | | |
|---|---|---|---|---|---|---|
| **750 g** | large potatoes, scrubbed | **1¼ lb** | **2 tsp** | safflower oil | **2 tsp** |
| **1 tsp** | chili powder | **1 tsp** | **¼ tsp** | salt | **¼ tsp** |

Put a large baking sheet in the oven and preheat the oven to 240°C (475°F or Mark 9). Cut the potatoes lengthwise into slices about 1 cm (½ inch) thick. Cut each slice lengthwise into 1 cm (½ inch) strips and put them in a large bowl. Toss the strips with the chili powder to coat them evenly; sprinkle on the oil and toss again.

Arrange the potato strips in a single layer on the hot baking sheet. Bake the strips for 20 minutes, then turn them and continue baking until they are crisp and browned—about 20 minutes more. Sprinkle the French fries with the salt and serve them hot.

# Grilled Entrecôte Steaks with Fennel-Scented Vegetables

**Serves 8**

**Working time:**
about 20
minutes

**Total time:**
about 40
minutes

**Calories**
235
**Protein**
26g
**Cholesterol**
65mg
**Total fat**
10g
**Saturated fat**
39g
**Sodium**
200g

| | | |
|---|---|---|
| 4 | thick entrecôte steaks (about 300 g/10 oz each), trimmed of fat | 4 |
| 2 tbsp | olive oil | 2 tbsp |
| 1½ tsp | fennel seeds, lightly crushed | 1½ tsp |
| 500 g | aubergine, cut into 1 cm (½ inch) cubes | 1 lb |

| | | |
|---|---|---|
| 175 g | onion, chopped | 6 oz |
| 2 tbsp | fresh lemon juice | 2 tbsp |
| 750 g | ripe tomatoes, skinned, seeded and cut into pieces | 1½ lb |
| ½ tsp | salt | ½ tsp |
| | freshly ground black pepper | |
| 3 | garlic cloves, very thinly sliced | 3 |

If you plan to grill the steaks preheat the grill for about 10 minutes before cooking.

In the meantime, heat the olive oil in a large, heavy frying pan over high heat. When the oil is hot, add the fennel seeds and garlic, and cook them for 30 seconds, stirring constantly. Add the aubergine, onion and lemon juice and cook the vegetables for 5 minutes, stirring frequently. Next, add the tomatoes, ¼ teaspoon of the salt and a generous grinding of pepper to the pan. Cook the vegetable mixture for 3 to 4 minutes

longer, stirring continuously. Cover the pan and set the mixture aside while you finish the dish.

Grill the steaks for 3 to 4 minutes. Turn the steaks over and sprinkle them with the remaining ¼ teaspoon of salt and some pepper. Cook the steaks for an additional 3 to 4 minutes for medium-rare meat. Let the steaks stand for 5 minutes before thinly slicing them against the grain. Divide the meat and vegetables among eight dinner plates and serve at once.

# White Cabbage Pork

| | | |
|---|---|---|
| Serves 4 | | |
| Working time: about 30 minutes | | |
| Total time: about 7 hours and 30 minutes (includes marinating) | | |

| | | |
|---|---|---|
| Calories 250 | | |
| Protein 23g | | |
| Cholesterol 70mg | | |
| Total fat 11g | | |
| Saturated fat 3g | | |
| Sodium 185mg | | |

| | | | |
|---|---|---|---|
| 500 g | boned pork loin, trimmed of fat | 1 lb | |
| 1½ tsp | caraway seeds | 1½ tsp | |
| 30 cl | apple juice | ½ pint | |
| 1 tbsp | safflower oil | 1 tbsp | |
| 1 | small onion, finely chopped | 1 | |
| 400 g | white cabbage, shredded | 14 oz | |
| ¼ tsp | salt | ¼ tsp | |
| | white pepper | | |
| 1 | small red-skinned apple, for garnish | 1 | |
| | dill sprigs, for garnish | | |

Sprinkle half the caraway seeds over the inside of the pork, roll it up and tie it with string. Place the pork in a non-reactive bowl, sprinkle the remaining caraway seeds over, then pour in the apple juice. Cover and leave in a cool place for 6 hours, turning occasionally.

Preheat the oven to 170°C (325°F or Mark 3).

Remove the pork from the bowl and pat it dry; reserve the apple juice. Heat a heavy fireproof casserole, add the oil and brown the pork evenly over high heat. Transfer to a plate. Add the onion and cook gently for 3 to 4 minutes. Add the cabbage in batches and cook each batch, stirring frequently, for 2 to 3

minutes; remove each batch in turn to a large bowl. When all the cabbage is cooked, stir the contents of the bowl to distribute the onion evenly. Set the pork on a layer of cabbage and onion in the casserole and surround it with the remaining cabbage and onion. Bring the reserved apple juice to the boil, season, then pour it over the pork.

Cover tightly and cook in the oven until the pork is tender—about 45 minutes. Transfer to a warmed plate, cover and leave for about 10 minutes. Meanwhile slice the apple.

Carve the pork into slices. Arrange the cabbage on a warm dish, place the pork on top and spoon the cooking juices over. Garnish with the dill and apple.

# Blackberry-Peach Crumble

Serves 8

Working time: about 30 minutes

Total time: about 1 hour and 15 minutes

Calories 175
Protein 3g
Cholesterol 30mg
Total fat 3g
Saturated fat 1g
Sodium 200mg

| | | | | | |
|---|---|---|---|---|---|
| 6 | ripe peaches | 6 | 1 tsp | baking powder | 1 tsp |
| 1 tbsp | fresh lemon juice | 1 tbsp | ¼ tsp | salt | ¼ tsp |
| 4 tbsp | sugar | 4 tbsp | 15 g | cold unsalted butter | ½ oz |
| 500 g | blackberries, picked over and stemmed, or other berries in season | 1 lb | 125 g | caster sugar | 4 oz |
| | **Crumble topping** | | 1 | egg | 1 |
| 90 g | wholemeal flour | 3 oz | ½ tsp | ground cinnamon | ½ tsp |
| | | | 1 tbsp | wheat germ | 1 tbsp |

Preheat the oven to 190°C (375°F or Mark 5).

Blanch the peaches in boiling water until their skins loosen—30 seconds to 1 minute. Peel the peaches and halve them lengthwise, discarding the stones. Cut each peach half into five or six slices. Put the slices in a bowl, add the lemon juice and sugar, and gently toss them together. Set aside.

To prepare the crumble topping, put the flour, baking powder, salt, butter and 100 g (3 ½ oz) of the sugar into a food processor; mix the ingredients just long enough to produce a fine-meal texture. Alternatively, put the dry ingredients into a bowl and cut the butter in

using a pastry blender or two knives. Add the egg and blend it in—5 to 10 seconds. The topping should have the texture of large crumbs.

Arrange the peach slices in an even layer in a large, shallow baking dish. Scatter the blackberries over the peach slices, then sprinkle the topping over the blackberries. Stir together the cinnamon, wheat germ and the remaining sugar, and strew this mixture over the crumble topping. Bake the dish until the topping is brown and the juices bubble up around the edges—45 to 55 minutes.

# Braised Steak with Onions

**Serves 6**

**Working time: about 1 hour**

**Total time: about 2 hours and 30 minutes**

**Calories 175**

**Protein 22g**

**Cholesterol 50mg**

**Total fat 5g**

**Saturated fat 2g**

**Sodium 195mg**

| | | |
|---|---|---|
| **850 g** | topside of beef, trimmed of fat and cut into six steaks | **1¾ lb** |
| **2 tsp** | safflower oil | **2 tsp** |
| **2** | large onions, thinly sliced | **2** |
| **½ litre** | red wine | **16 fl oz** |
| **2** | carrots, cut into batonnets | **2** |
| **1** | stick celery, chopped | **1** |
| **¼ tsp** | salt | **¼ tsp** |
| | freshly ground black pepper | |
| **½ litre** | unsalted brown stock | **16 fl oz** |

Preheat the oven to 170°C (325°F or Mark 3).

Heat the oil in a large, shallow fireproof casserole over medium heat. Add the onions and cook them, stirring frequently, until they are translucent and their juices have caramelized—5 to 10 minutes. Pour 12.5 cl (4 fl oz) of the wine into the casserole, increase the heat, and boil the wine until nearly all the liquid has evaporated. Add in another 12.5 cl (4 fl oz) and reduce this also.

Boil away the remaining wine in two batches, stirring constantly as the last batch begins to evaporate.

Add the carrots, celery, salt, some pepper and the stock to the casserole. Lay the steaks on top of the vegetables; cover the casserole and transfer it to the oven. Braise the steaks until they are tender—1½ to 2 hours. Serve the steaks topped with the vegetables and braising juices.

# Salade Niçoise

Serves 4 as a
main course

Working time:
about 30
minutes

Total time:
about 1 hour
and 45
minutes

Calories
380
Protein
35g
Cholesterol
45mg
Total fat
13g
Saturated fat
2g
Sodium
210mg

| | | |
|---|---|---:|
| 500 g | small round red potatoes | 1 lb |
| 250 g | French beans, trimmed | 8 oz |
| 3 | oil-cured black olives, stoned and coarsely chopped | 3 |
| 250 g | ripe tomatoes, cored and sliced | 8 oz |
| 2 | hard-boiled egg whites chopped | 2 |
| 2 tbsp | white wine vinegar | 2 tbsp |
| 2 tbsp | chopped fresh tarragon | 2 tbsp |
| 2 tsp | Dijon mustard | 2 tsp |

| | | |
|---|---|---:|
| 1 | small red onion, peeled, sliced and separated into rings | 1 |
| 1 | garlic clove, finely chopped | 1 |
| 6 tbsp | fish stock | 6 tbsp |
| | freshly ground black pepper | |
| 500 g | raw tuna fillet, cut into 1 cm (½ inch) wide strips | 1 lb |
| 1 tbsp | virgin olive oil | 1 tbsp |
| 2 | round lettuces, washed and dried | 2 |

Prick the potatoes with a fork in two places. Arrange them in a circle on paper towels in the microwave and cook on high for 4 minutes. Turn the potatoes over and cook until barely tender—3 to 4 minutes more.

Put the beans in a bowl and pour in 4 tablespoons of water. Cover and microwave on high until tender but still crisp—3 to 4 minutes. Drain and refresh, then transfer them to a salad bowl. Peel the potatoes and cut them into small chunks. Add the potatoes, olives, tomatoes and egg whites to the beans.

Combine the vinegar, tarragon, mustard, onion, garlic, stock and some pepper in a bowl. Cook the mixture on high until it boils—about 3 minutes. Remove the bowl from the oven. Rinse the tuna, pat it dry, and add it to the bowl. Mix well, then cover the bowl tightly, and set it aside for 3 minutes. The tuna should be opaque and firm; if not, reheat the liquid, and steep the tuna again.

Add the cooked tuna and its steeping liquid to the salad. Pour in the oil and toss the gently. Refrigerate for 45 minutes. Serve on a bed of lettuce.

# Lamb Paprika

**Serves 4**

**Working time: about 25 minutes**

**Total time: about 6 hours and 25 minutes (includes marinating)**

**Calories 245**

**Protein 30g**

**Cholesterol 85mg**

**Total fat 11g**

**Saturated fat 5g**

**Sodium 350mg**

| | | |
|---|---|---|
| **500 g** | lean lamb (from the fillet end of the leg), trimmed of fat and cut into thin strips | **1 lb** |
| **1 tbsp** | paprika | **1 tbsp** |
| **¼ tsp** | freshly ground black pepper | **¼ tsp** |
| **½ tsp** | salt | **½ tsp** |
| **350 g** | kale, washed, stemmed and chopped | **12 oz** |
| **2 tsp** | caraway seeds | **2 tsp** |
| **15 g** | polyunsaturated marganne | **½ oz** |
| **1** | garlic clove, crushed | **1** |
| **3** | shallots, thinly sliced | **3** |
| **2** | bay leaves | **2** |
| **3** | tomatoes, skinned and chopped | **3** |
| **3 tbsp** | medium-dry sherry | **3 tbsp** |
| **2 tbsp** | soured cream | **2 tbsp** |

Put the lamb in a bowl with the paprika, the pepper and half of the salt, and stir until the meat is evenly coated. Cover the bowl and leave it in a cool place to marinate for at least 6 hours or overnight. Stir the meat once during this period.

Pour enough water into a large saucepan to fill it about 2.5 cm (1 inch) deep. Place a vegetable steamer in the pan and bring the water to the boil. Put the chopped kale in the steamer and sprinkle it with the remaining salt and the caraway seeds. Cover the saucepan and cook until the kale is just tender and bright green—5 to 6 minutes.

Meanwhile, melt the margarine in a large, heavy frying pan. Stir in the garlic, shallots and bay leaves and cook them over medium heat until the shallots are softened—1 to 2 minutes. Increase the heat to high and sauté the lamb, stirring occasionally, until it has changed colour all over—2 to 3 minutes. Stir in the tomatoes and sherry. Bring the mixture to the boil and cook it for 2 minutes.

Spoon the kale into a hot serving dish, cover it and keep it warm. Transfer the lamb and its sauce to a second hot dish, stir in the soured cream and serve immediately, accompanied by the kale.

# Useful weights and measures

## Weight Equivalents

| Avoirdupois | | Metric |
|---|---|---|
| 1 ounce | = | 28.35 grams |
| 1 pound | = | 254.6 grams |
| 2.3 pounds | = | 1 kilogram |

## Liquid Measurements

| | | |
|---|---|---|
| $^1/_4$ pint | = | $1^1/_2$ decilitres |
| $^1/_2$ pint | = | $^1/_4$ litre |
| scant 1 pint | = | $^1/_2$ litre |
| $1^3/_4$ pints | = | 1 litre |
| 1 gallon | = | 4.5 litres |

## Liquid Measures

| | | | | |
|---|---|---|---|---|
| 1 pint | = 20 fl oz | = 32 tablespoons |
| $^1/_2$ pint | = 10 fl oz | = 16 tablespoons |
| $^1/_4$ pint | = 5 fl oz | = 8 tablespoons |
| $^1/_8$ pint | = $2^1/_2$ fl oz | = 4 tablespoons |
| $^1/_{16}$ pint | = $1^1/_4$ fl oz | = 2 tablespoons |

## Solid Measures

1 oz almonds, ground = $3^3/_4$ level tablespoons

1 oz breadcrumbs fresh = 7 level tablespoons

1 oz butter, lard = 2 level tablespoons

1 oz cheese, grated = $3^1/_2$ level tablespoons

1 oz cocoa = $2^3/_4$ level tablespoons

1 oz desiccated coconut = $4^1/_2$ tablespoons

1 oz cornflour = $2^1/_2$ tablespoons

1 oz custard powder = $2^1/_2$ tablespoons

1 oz curry powder and spices = 5 tablespoons

1 oz flour = 2 level tablespoons

1 oz rice, uncooked = $1^1/_2$ tablespoons

1 oz sugar, caster and granulated = 2 tablespoons

1 oz icing sugar = $2^1/_2$ tablespoons

1 oz yeast, granulated = 1 level tablespoon

## American Measures

| | |
|---|---|
| 16 fl oz | =1 American pint |
| 8 fl oz | =1 American standard cup |
| 0.50 fl oz | =1 American tablespoon |

(*slightly smaller than British Standards Institute tablespoon*)

| | |
|---|---|
| 0.16 fl oz | =1 American teaspoon |

## Australian Cup Measures

(*Using the 8-liquid-ounce cup measure*)

| | |
|---|---|
| 1 cup flour | 4 oz |
| 1 cup sugar (crystal or caster) | 8 oz |
| 1 cup icing sugar (free from lumps) | 5 oz |
| 1 cup shortening (butter, margarine) | 8 oz |
| 1 cup brown sugar (lightly packed) | 4 oz |
| 1 cup soft breadcrumbs | 2 oz |
| 1 cup dry breadcrumbs | 3 oz |
| 1 cup rice (uncooked) | 6 oz |
| 1 cup rice (cooked) | 5 oz |
| 1 cup mixed fruit | 4 oz |
| 1 cup grated cheese | 4 oz |
| 1 cup nuts (chopped) | 4 oz |
| 1 cup coconut | $2^1/_2$ oz |

## Australian Spoon Measures

| | *level tablespoon* |
|---|---|
| 1 oz flour | 2 |
| 1 oz sugar | $1^1/_2$ |
| 1 oz icing sugar | 2 |
| 1 oz shortening | 1 |
| 1 oz honey | 1 |
| 1 oz gelatine | 2 |
| 1 oz cocoa | 3 |
| 1 oz cornflour | $2^1/_2$ |
| 1 oz custard powder | $2^1/_2$ |

## Australian Liquid Measures

(*Using 8-liquid-ounce cup*)

| | |
|---|---|
| 1 cup liquid | 8 oz |
| $2^1/_2$ cups liquid | 20 oz (1 pint) |
| 2 tablespoons liquid | 1 oz |
| 1 gill liquid | 5 oz ($^1/_4$ pint) |